**MARYLAND &
WASHINGTON, D.C.**

W9-AVN-378

□ NATIONAL GEOGRAPHIC

FIELD GUIDE TO

BIRDS

MARYLAND &
WASHINGTON, D.C.

 NATIONAL GEOGRAPHIC

FIELD GUIDE TO
BIRDS

Edited by JONATHAN ALDERFER

National Geographic
Washington, D.C.

Introduction

The small state of Maryland is a virtual transect of East Coast habitats. Maryland's coast includes 30 miles of barrier-island dunes and beachfront, more than half of it undeveloped. Inland, the Coastal Plain is a patchwork of woodland and agriculture, though the many tributaries of the Chesapeake Bay support extensive salt and fresh marshes. The bay itself, the largest estuary in the country, is a mecca for bird life, hosting more than 30 species of wintering waterfowl alone. From the coastal plain, one climbs onto the Piedmont, a more hilly and rocky section of the state that begins just about at the Baltimore-Washington Parkway. Broad-winged Hawks and Common Nighthawks migrate along this corridor on clear September days. From Frederick County west to Frostburg, linear ridges dominate the landscape, their forested peaks home to Ruffed Grouse and Common Ravens. Finally, Garrett County, atop the Allegheny Plateau, is highlighted by 29 species of breeding warblers. The diversity of habitats in Maryland supports 427 species of birds, of which 216 are known to breed.

Even the District of Columbia, covering just 69 square miles (8 square miles of which is water) and almost completely urban, has recorded some 325 species of birds. The Potomac River is still tidal in southern D. C. off Hains Point, and is good for waterfowl. Rock Creek Park is renowned as a migration hot spot amid a sea of humanity. It is possible to see 10 flycatchers, 6 vireos, or 25 species of warblers there on a perfect migration day.

May you have this book in your pocket on the next perfect migration day in Maryland or Washington, D. C.

MARSHALL J. ILIFF
PAST REGIONAL EDITOR
North American Birds

FRONTISPIECE: BALTIMORE ORIOLE
PHOTO BY ALAN MURPHY

CONTENTS

P E N N S

ROCKY GAP
S.P.

Hancock

APPALACHIAN
NATIONAL
SCENIC TRAIL

NEW
GERMANY
S.P.

Frostburg

CATOCTIN MOUNTAIN
PARK

• Cumberland

WASHINGTON
MONUMENT

W. VA.

Deep Creek
Lake

ANTIETAM N.B.
Sharpsburg •

S.P.

SWALLOW
FALLS
S.P.

Chesapeake and Ohio Canal

• Oakland

WEST

CHESAPEAKE &
OHIO CANAL
N.H.P.

• Frederick

Potomac

Backbone Mt.
3,360 ft+
1,024 m

VIRGINIA

Lilypons Water Gardens

Little Seneca Regional Park

SENECA CREEK S.

McKEE BESHERS W.M.A.

VIRGINIA

SELECTED BIRDING SITES OF
MARYLAND AND THE
DISTRICT OF COLUMBIA

MAP KEY

National Park, N.P.
National Historical Park, N.H.P.
National Historic Site, N.H.S.
National Memorial, NAT. MEM.
National Monument, NAT. MON.
State Park, S.P.
Wildlife Management Area, W.M.A.
National Wildlife Refuge, N.W.R.

State boundary

/ Dam

Canal

Abandoned Canal

– – Trail

⊛ State capital

◉ National capital

□ Point of interest

miles
0 _____ 50

0 _____ 50
kilometers

PENNSYLVANIA

Monocacy
Taneytown
Mason-Dixon Line
Conowingo Dam
Susquehanna
Westminster
Liberty Res.
Elkton
Chesapeake & Delaware Canal
Bel Air
Aberdeen
Loch Raven Reservoir
Baltimore
ELK NECK S.P.
Essex
Sassafras
Ellicott City
MARYLAND
Germantown
Columbia
Gaithersburg
Rockville
PATUXENT N.W.R.
SANDY POINT S.P.
Bethesda
Silver Spring
Severna Park
EASTERN NECK N.W.R.
ROCK CREEK PARK
Kent I.
DELAWARE
D.C. Washington
Annapolis
Eastern Bay
Choptank
PISCATAWAY PARK
Patuxent
Easton
DELAWARE
Chesapeake Beach
Waldorf
St. Charles
Choptank
La Plata
Prince Frederick
Chesapeake Bay
Cambridge
Nanticoke
Salisbury
Ocean City
BLACKWATER N.W.R.
Ocean City Inlet
Lexington Park
St. Marys City
Bloodsworth Island
Snow Hill
DEAL ISLAND W.M.A.
Potomac
Tangier Sound
Pocomoke City
DELMARVA PENINSULA
POINT LOOKOUT S.P.
GLENN MARTIN N.W.R.
Pocomoke
ASSATEAGUE I. NATIONAL SEASHORE
Point Lookout
Smith I.
E. A. VAUGHN W.M.A.
Chincoteague Bay
VIRGINIA
VA.
ATLANTIC OCEAN

LOOKING AT BIRDS

What do the artist and the nature lover share? A passion for being attuned to the world and all of its complexity, via the senses. Every time you go out into the natural world, or even view it through a window, you have another opportunity to see what is there. And the more you know what you are looking at, the more you see.

Even if you are not yet a committed birder, it makes sense to take a field guide with you when you go out for a walk or a hike. Looking for and identifying birds will sharpen and heighten your perceptions, and intensify your experience. And you'll find that you notice everything else more acutely—the terrain, the season, the weather, the plant life, other animal life.

Birds are beautiful, complex animals that live everywhere around us in our towns and cities and in distant places we dream of visiting. Here in North America more than 900 species have been recorded—from abundant commoners to the rare and exotic. A comprehensive field reference like the *National Geographic Field Guide to the Birds of North America* is essential for understanding that big picture. If you are taking a spring walk in Rock Creek Park, however, you may want something simpler: a guide to the birds you are most likely to see, which slips easily into a pocket.

This photographic guide is designed to provide an introduction to the common birds—and some of the specialty birds—you might encounter in Maryland and the District of Columbia: how to identify them, how they behave, and where to find them, with specific locations.

Discovery, observation, and identification of birds is exciting, whether you are novice or expert. I know that every time I go out to look at birds, I see more clearly and have a greater appreciation for the natural world and my own place in it.

JONATHAN ALDERFER
Editor

National Geographic Field Guide to Birds: Maryland and Washington, D.C. is designed to help beginning and practiced birders alike identify birds in the field and introduce them to the region's varied bird life. The book is organized by bird families, following the order in the *Checklist of North American Birds,* by the American Ornithologists' Union. Families share structural characteristics, and by learning these shared characteristics early, birders can establish a basis for a lifetime of identifying birds and related family members with great accuracy—sometimes merely at a glance. (For quick reference in the field, use the color and alphabetical indexes at the back of this book.)

A family may have one member or dozens of members, or species. In this book each family is identified by its common name in English along the right-hand border of each spread. Each species is also identified in English, with its Latin genus and species—its scientific name—found directly underneath. One species is featured in each entry.

eye ring
scapulars
median coverts
greater coverts
wing bar
flank
tertials
secondaries
primaries

Least Flycatcher

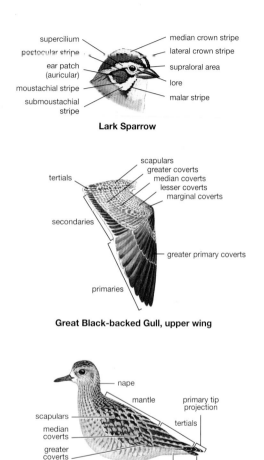

Lark Sparrow

supercilium
postocular stripe
ear patch (auricular)
moustachial stripe
submoustachial stripe

median crown stripe
lateral crown stripe
supraloral area
lore
malar stripe

Great Black-backed Gull, upper wing

scapulars
greater coverts
median coverts
lesser coverts
marginal coverts
tertials
secondaries
greater primary coverts
primaries

Pacific Golden-Plover

nape
mantle
primary tip projection
tertials
scapulars
median coverts
greater coverts
tail
tibia
tarsus
undertail coverts

An entry begins with **Field Marks,** the physical clues used to quickly identify a bird, such as body shape and size, bill length, and plumage color or pattern. A bird's body parts yield vital clues to identification, so a birder needs to become familiar with them early on. After the first glance at body type, take note of the head shape and markings, such as stripes, eye rings, and crown markings. Bill shape and color are important as well. Note body and wing details: wing bars, color of and pattern of wing feathers at rest, and shape and markings when extended in flight. Tail shape, length, color, and banding may play a big part, too. At left are diagrams detailing the various parts of a bird—its topography—labeled with the term likely to be found in the text of this book.

The main body of each entry is divided into three categories: Behavior, Habitat, and Local Sites. The **Behavior** section details certain characteristics to look or listen for in the field. Often a bird's behavioral characteristics are very closely related to its body type and field marks, such as in the case of woodpeckers, whose stiff tails, strong legs, and sharp claws enable them to spend most of their lives in an upright position, braced against a tree trunk. The **Habitat** section describes areas that are most likely to support the featured species. Preferred nesting locations of breeding birds are also included in many cases. The **Local Sites** section recommends specific refuges or parks where the featured bird is likely to be found. A section called **Field Notes** finishes each entry, and includes information such as plumage variations within a species; or it may introduce another species with which the featured bird is frequently confused. In either case, an additional drawing may be included to aid in identification.

Finally, a caption under each of the photographs gives the season of the plumage pictured, as well as the age and sex of the bird, if discernable. A key to using this informative guide and its range maps follows on the next two pages.

Rear-read | Adult male

The spread shows a Red-Bellied Woodpecker page with the following annotations:

RED-BELLIED WOODPECKER

Melanerpes carolinus L 9.3" (24 cm)

FIELD MARKS
Black-and-white barred back

Red nape, extending onto crown only on males

Mostly grayish underparts; small reddish tinge on belly

Central tail feathers barred

Behavior
Climbs tree trunks by bracing itself with stiff tail, taking strain off short legs. Uses chisel-shaped bill to drill cavities in tree bark for nest holes and to extract grubs and insects. Also feeds on worms, fruits, seeds, and sap. Will use backyard feeders for sunflower seeds and peanut butter. Nests and roosts at night in tree cavities. Call during breeding season is a rolling *churrr.* Also gives a conversational *chiv chiv* all year.

Habitat
Common in open woodlands, forest edges, suburbs, and parks.

Local Sites
These conspicuous residents are common in cities,sub-urbs, parks, and woodlands throughout Maryland. Rock Creek Park is the best place to see it within D. C.

FIELD NOTES — Red-headed Woodpecker, *Melanerpes...* shares much of the Red-bellied's range, but is much leaner. The adult Red-bellied is identified by its bright red hood and its stark white rump and underparts. The juvenile has a brownish hood and back.

---

❶ **Photograph:** Shows bird in habitat. May be female or male, adult or juvenile. Plumage may be breeding, molting, nonbreeding, or year-round.

❷ **Caption:** Defines the featured bird's plumage, age, and sometimes sex, as seen in the picture.

❸ **Heading:** Beneath the common name find the Latin, or scientific, name. Beside it is the bird's length (L), and sometimes its wingspan (WS). Wingspan is given with birds often seen in flight. Female measurements are given if noticeably different from male.

❹ **Field Marks:** Gives basic facts for field identification: markings, head and bill shape, and body size.

❺ **Band:** Gives the common name of the bird's family.

❻ **Range Map:** Shows year-round range in purple, breeding range in red, winter range in blue. Areas through which species are likely to migrate are shown in green.

❼ **Behavior:** A step beyond **Field Marks,** gives clues to identifying a bird by its habits, such as feeding, flight pattern, courtship, nest-building, or songs and calls.

❽ **Habitat:** Reveals the area a species is most likely to inhabit, such as forests, marshes, grasslands, or urban areas. May include preferred nesting sites.

❾ **Local Sites:** Details local spots to look for the given species.

❿ **Field Notes:** A special entry that may give a unique point of identification, compare two species of the same family, compare two species from different families that are easily confused, or focus on a historical or conservation fact.

On each map of Maryland and D.C., range boundaries are drawn beyond which the species is not regularly seen. Nearly every species will be rare at the edges of its range. The sample map shown below explains the colors and symbols used on each map. Ranges continually expand and contract, so the map is a tool, not a rule. Range information is based on actual sightings and therefore depends upon the number of knowledgeable and active birders in each area.

Map Key

Breeding range, generally in spring and summer

Winter range

Year-round range

Migration range

Sample Map: Savannah Sparrow

READING THE INDEXES

There are two indexes at the back of this book. The first is a **Color Index** (p. 262), created to help birders quickly find an entry by noting its color in the field. In this index, male birds are labeled by their predominant color: Mostly White, Mostly Black, etc. Note that a bird may have a head of a different color than its label states. That's because its body—the part most noticeable in the field—is the color labeled.

The **Alphabetical Index** (p. 266) is organized by the bird's common name. Next to each entry is a check-off box. Most birders make lists of the birds they see. Some keep several lists, perhaps one of birds in a certain area and another of all the birds they've ever seen—a life list. Such lists enable birders to look back and remember their first sighting of an Indigo Bunting or an American Kestrel.

Year-round | Adult white morph

SNOW GOOSE

Chen caerulescens L 31" (79 cm) WS 56" (142 cm)

FIELD MARKS

White overall

Black primaries show in flight

Heavy pinkish bill with black "grinning patch"

Juvenile is dingy gray-brown on head, neck, and upperparts

Behavior
Travels in large flocks, especially during spring migration. Loud, vocal birds that sound like baying hounds, flocks migrate in loose V-formation and long lines, sometimes more than 1,500 miles nonstop, reaching speeds up to 40 mph. Primarily vegetarian, forages on agricultural grains and plants and aquatic vegetation. An agile swimmer, commonly rests on water during migration and at wintering grounds. Listen for its harsh, descending *whouk*, heard continuously in flight.

Habitat
Most often seen on grasslands, grainfields, and wetlands, favoring standing shallow freshwater marshes and flooded fields. Breeds in the Arctic.

Local Sites
Blackwater National Wildlife Refuge is one of several places on the Eastern Shore where this species is easily seen. Thousands congregate from October to March, including a high proportion of dark morphs.

FIELD NOTES Amid a flock of white Snow Geese, you may see a few dark morphs as well, characterized by a varying amount of dark gray-brown on the back and breast (inset). These birds were formerly considered a separate species, the Blue Goose.

Immature

BRANT

Branta bernicla L 25" (64 cm)

FIELD MARKS

Small, dark, and stocky with
black head, neck, breast, and bill

Distinctive whitish patch on each
side of neck

White uppertail coverts and black
tail conspicuous in flight

Behavior

Flocks fly low in ragged formations with no evident
lead bird. The Brant rests near open water and waits for
a falling tide to trigger its appetite. Though some
populations have adapted to wintering on grassy fields,
the birds continue to forage during low tide in nearby
bays, and lift off for the fields as the tide begins to rise.
Call is a low, rolling, throaty *raunk-raunk*.

Habitat

The Brant winters along sea coasts, feeding on the
aquatic plants of shallow bays and estuaries. It breeds
on Arctic tundra, and tends to build its nest of grass
and other materials on small islands one to five miles
from the coast.

Local Sites

Brants are best seen in downtown Ocean City, where
they graze on athletic fields or rest and feed in
Assawoman Bay. Ocean City Inlet and Skimmer Island
(off 4th Street, bayside) are good locations.

FIELD NOTES This species experienced a great decline in number
in the 1930s due to a scarcity of eelgrass, its favored food at the
time. Brants adapted to other aquatic vegetation and winter
grainfields to survive, and the species has rebounded.

Year-round | Adult

CANADA GOOSE

Branta canadensis L 30-43" (75-108 cm) WS 59-73" (148-183 cm)

FIELD MARKS

Black head and neck marked with distinctive white chin strap

In flight, shows large, dark wings, white undertail coverts, and a long protruding neck

Brown body, paler below; white vent and belly

Behavior

A common, familiar goose; best known for migrating in large V-formation. Like some other members of its family, finds a mate and is monogamous for life. Nests on the ground in open or forested areas near water. Its distinctive honking call is easy to identify. Males give a lower-pitched *hwonk,* females a higher *hrink.*

Habitat

Prefers wetlands, grasslands, and cultivated fields within commuting distance of water. Introduced birds have become resident and have adapted successfully to man-made habitats such as golf courses, landscaped ponds, and farms.

Local Sites

Virtually every lake and pond in Maryland and D.C. hosts year-round residents. Thousands of migrants visit Blackwater and Eastern Neck National Wildlife Refuges.

FIELD NOTES Research into the mitochondrial DNA of the Canada Goose has revealed that the smaller subspecies, such as *hutchinsii* (inset, left) and *minima* (inset, right), actually belong to their own species, the newly named Cackling Goose, *Branta hutchinsii,* which is rare in Maryland and D.C.

Year-round | Adults

TUNDRA SWAN

Cygnus columbianus L 52" (132 cm)

FIELD MARKS
White overall

Black, slightly concave bill with yellow spot of variable size in front of eye

Juvenile appears darker with pinkish bill

Behavior
Feeds on aquatic vegetation in shallow water, its long neck enabling it to keep its body upright. Flies in straight lines or in V-formation, with its neck protruding forward. Following the same routes every year, the Tundra Swan migrates thousands of miles between Arctic breeding grounds and temperate wintering quarters. Call is a noisy, barking *kwooo,* often heard at night.

Habitat
Winters in coastal areas on ponds, lakes, estuaries, and marshes. Breeds on ponds in Alaska and the Arctic.

Local Sites
Eastern Neck National Wildlife Refuge and West Ocean City Park host flocks of Tundra Swans regularly in winter. During November and March, flocks may fly over any part of the state, often at night when their calls betray their passage.

FIELD NOTES Tundra Swans wintering in the Chesapeake Bay region appear to have changed their diet significantly in the past century. Where they once fed primarily on aquatic grasses, the depletion of grass beds and the abundance of spilled grain have led to a shift to feeding in farm fields and the addition of clams and other mollusks to their estuarine foraging.

Year-round | Adult

MUTE SWAN

Cygnus olor L 60" (152 cm)

FIELD MARKS

White overall; orange bill with
black knob at base

Fluffy back feathers

Juvenile gray with dull gray bill

Behavior

Native to Europe and Asia, this showy swan has been
stocked at city parks around the world. Feeds primarily
on aquatic grasses in shallow water, its long neck
enabling it to keep its body upright. Builds nest in
grassy areas along the water's edge. Most often in pairs,
although flocks may gather to molt and to spend the
winter. Nonmigratory, its flights are typically short and
at low altitude. Emits grunts and hisses near nest site;
its wings make loud whistle in flight.

Habitat

The many creeks and coves of Chesapeake Bay are ideal
habitat for the Mute Swan. Flocks gather in winter at
favored feeding areas.

Local Sites

Easily found at Eastern Neck National Wildlife Refuge
or on Kent Island, including ponds at the east end of
the Bay Bridge.

FIELD NOTES In 1962, an escaped Mute Swan pair bred successfully, and it is thought that the entire Chesapeake Bay population
originated with those two birds. Now widespread and continuing
to expand, Mute Swans are a pest species in the Chesapeake;
they destroy aquatic grasses vital to the health of the bay and
are aggressive toward other birds.

Breeding | Adult male

WOOD DUCK

Aix sponsa L 18.5" (47 cm)

FIELD MARKS

Male has glossy iridescent head and crest, lined in white; red, white, black, and yellow bill; burgundy breast with white spotting; yellowish sides

Female duller overall with large white teardrop-shaped eye patch

Behavior

Most commonly feeds by picking insects from the water's surface or by tipping into shallows to pluck invertebrates from the bottom, but may also be seen foraging on land. The omnivorous Wood Duck's diet changes throughout the year depending upon available foods and its need for particular proteins or minerals during migration, breeding, and molting. Nests in tree cavities or man-made nest boxes. Male Wood Ducks give a soft, upslurred whistle when swimming. Female Wood Ducks have a distinctive rising, squealing flight call of *ooEEK*.

Habitat

Inhabits woodlands and forested swamps.

Local Sites

Common along wooded rivers, and especially beaver swamps, the Wood Duck can be found at Hughes Hollow, Patuxent Research Refuge, or the Pocomoke River.

FIELD NOTES The Wood Duck female (inset) hatches up to 15 eggs in cavities high up in trees or nest boxes. Once hatched, the young must make a long jump to the water, sometimes 30 feet below. Protected by their downy plumage, they generally land safely.

Breeding | Adult male

AMERICAN WIGEON

Anas americana L 19" (48 cm)

FIELD MARKS
White cap and forehead on male; green patch extending back from eyes; white wing patch

Both sexes have large white patch on underwing

Rusty brown chest, flanks, and back; white belly; pointed tail

Behavior
Grazes in fields and was once considered an agricultural pest. Often feeds in shallow water with other duck species; has also been known to forage in deeper waters, and to steal food from diving ducks or coots. Flushes readily if disturbed. Tight flocks careen together impressively. Male's whistle is a three-note *whew-whew-whew;* female gives off a low, harsh quack.

Habitat
Found in various wetland habitats, ranging from marshes to lakes, bays, coastal estuaries, flooded fields, and even golf courses. The American Wigeon's shallow nest is built on dry land among tall weeds.

Local Sites
Many coastal bays, lakes, and ponds that host waterfowl may have wigeons in winter or during migration. Eastern Neck National Wildlife Refuge and West Ocean City Pond are two especially good sites.

FIELD NOTES The Gadwall, *Anas strepera* (inset: female, left; male, right), is a common migrant and winter resident regionwide, and an uncommon breeder in salt marshes. Female resembles female Mallard (pages 30-31), but bill has orange only on the sides.

Year-round | Male

AMERICAN BLACK DUCK

Anas rubripes L 23" (58 cm)

FIELD MARKS

Blackish brown body, paler on
face and foreneck

In flight, white wing linings
contrast sharply with dark body;
violet speculum bordered in black

Male's bill is yellow, female's is
dull green

Behavior

Feeds in shallow water, mostly on aquatic vegetation in
winter and aquatic insects in summer. Female builds
nest of plant material and downy feathers in a shallow
depression on the ground. The female Black Duck gives
a typical loud *QUACK;* the male's call is shorter and
lower-pitched.

Habitat

Found in woodland lakes and streams and in coastal
marshes, often in the company of Mallards (next page).

Local Sites

American Black Ducks are found regionwide in winter
on ponds and lakes, but are most common in coastal
salt marshes. Look for them throughout the year at
Blackwater National Wildlife Refuge or Deal Island
Wildlife Management Area.

FIELD NOTES The American Black Duck population seems to be
losing ground due to increased deforestation and displacement
by the highly adaptable Mallard, with which the Black Duck often
hybridizes. The female Mallard (inset) closely
resembles the American Black Duck. Look
for her warmer brown body, orange bill with
dark center, and blue speculum bordered in
white. Hybrids are uncommon and may
look like American Black Ducks with whitish
tails and patches of green on the head.

Breeding | Adult male

MALLARD

Anas platyrhynchos L 23" (58 cm)

FIELD MARKS

Male has metallic green head and
neck; white collar; chestnut breast

Female mottled brown overall;
orange bill marked with black

Both sexes have bright blue
speculum bordered in white; white
tail and underwings

Behavior

A dabbler, the Mallard feeds by "tipping up" in shallow
water, plucking seeds, grasses, and invertebrates from
the bottom. Also picks insects from the water's surface.
Courtship ritual consists of the male pumping his
head, dipping his bill, and rearing up in the water to
exaggerate his size. A female signals consent by dupli-
cating the male's head-pumping. Nests on the ground
in concealing vegetation. The female is known for her
loud, descending *QUACK*. The male's call is shorter,
softer, less commonly given.

Habitat

Occurs wherever shallow fresh water is found, from
rural swamps to city ponds.

Local Sites

Look for Mallards at almost any lake, river, or other
wetland. Large numbers gather in winter
at Blackwater N. W. R.

FIELD NOTES At first glance,
the bright green head of the male
Northern Shoveler, *Anas clypeata*
(inset: female, left; male, right), can be mistaken for the
Mallard's. Look for the shoveler's large, dark, spatulate bill—a
telltale mark on both sexes. The Northern Shoveler winters
regularly on Maryland's Eastern Shore.

Breeding | Adult male

CANVASBACK

Aythya valisineria L 21" (53 cm)

FIELD MARKS

Male's head and neck are chestnut; back and sides whitish; breast and tail black

Female's head, neck, and breast are pale brown; back and sides pale gray

Forehead slopes to long, black bill

Behavior
Feeds on the water in large flocks, diving deep for fish, mollusks, and vegetation. Its heavy body requires a running start on water for takeoff. Flocks fly fairly high in lines or in irregular V-formation. Walks awkwardly, but not often seen on land. Both sexes are generally silent.

Habitat
Found in marshes, on lakes, and along rivers. Breeds in thick marsh grasses on upper Great Plains and north through Canada to Alaska, where it is a frequent victim of brood parasitism by the closely related Redhead.

Local Sites
Chesapeake Bay is an essential wintering location for this declining duck species. Flocks winter along the Cambridge waterfront, at West Ocean City pond, at Chesapeake Beach, and around Annapolis, especially near Thomas Point.

FIELD NOTES Sharing the male Canvasback's rufous head and neck, the male Redhead, *Aythya americana* (inset), can be difficult to distinguish in the field. Look for its grayer back, tricolored bill of pale blue, white, and black, and yellow eyes—the Canvasback's eyes are red. Large flocks of Canvasbacks in Maryland usually host one or more Redheads as well.

Breeding | Adult male

LESSER SCAUP

Aythya affinis L 16.5" (42 cm)

FIELD MARKS

Black head is slightly peaked, sometimes with purplish gloss

Black neck and breast, black tail; black-and-white barred back; white sides

Female has brown head, neck, upperparts; white at base of bill

Behavior

One of North America's most abundant diving ducks perhaps due to its omnivorous diet. Forages for aquatic insects, mollusks, snails, leeches, crustaceans, and small fish. Dives to sift through mud for seeds and aquatic vegetation. Both sexes are generally silent. Breeds in western prairie marshes.

Habitat

Large flocks can be found in winter in sheltered bays, inlets, lakes, and rivers. Some birds may also wander farther afield to agricultural fields and marshes.

Local Sites

Small numbers may turn up in migration at lakes and ponds regionwide. Wintering birds are widespread in sheltered coves of Chesapeake Bay. Try Eastern Neck N. W. R. or the Cambridge or Chesapeake Beach waterfronts.

FIELD NOTES The Greater Scaup, *Aythya marila* (inset: male, left; female, right), very closely resembles the Lesser in both sexes. The Greater's more rounded head is its most distinguishable field mark. The larger amount of white on the Greater Scaup's wings is another helpful field mark. Greater Scaup mixes with Lesser Scaup on Chesapeake Bay (but is rare inland), affording good opportunities for comparison.

Year-round | Adult male

SURF SCOTER

Melanitta perspicillata L 20" (51 cm)

FIELD MARKS

Male black overall, bold white forehead and nape patch; black, white, red, and yellow bill

Female brown with two white patches on each side of head

Distinctly sloping forehead

Behavior

A true sea duck found wintering in Chesapeake Bay and along the coast. Forages by diving, mainly for mollusks such as clams and mussels. Large flocks assemble at favorable feeding locations, particularly at low tide when food is more accessible. Bold black-and-white head pattern earned this elegant duck the inappropriate sobriquet of "skunkhead." Though usually silent, sometimes emits low-pitched, gurgling notes.

Habitat

Large flocks winter along the coast in shallow marine water or in coastal bays and sounds. Breeds on the subarctic tundra.

Local Sites

The most common scoter in Chesapeake Bay. Point Lookout State Park is a good place to see them; try also Chesapeake Beach, Cambridge, or Ocean City Inlet.

FIELD NOTES Two other scoters share the Surf Scoter's wintering grounds, the White-winged Scoter, *Melanitta fusca,* identifiable by its black plumage, white wing patch, and the male's spot of white by his eye; and the Black Scoter, *Melanitta nigra* (inset: male). The male Black Scoter is all black with a bright yellow-orange knob on its otherwise black bill; the female resembles an American Black Duck (pages 28-29), but has an all-dark bill.

Nonbreeding | Adult male

LONG-TAILED DUCK

Clangula hyemalis Male L 22" (56 cm) Female L 16" (41 cm)

FIELD MARKS

Winter male is largely white; breast and back blackish; stubby bill shows pink band

Female has white underparts, dark upperparts, and cheek patch

Male's long, black tail conspicuous in flight

Behavior
Tightly packed flocks careen low over the ocean as they move from place to place in winter. The Long-tailed Duck dives to forage at depths down to 200 feet. Can be identified by its loud, yodeling, segmented call of *ow-ow-owdle-ow*, which can be heard any time of the year from up to a mile away. The female also grunts and quacks from late winter through spring.

Habitat
Winters along coasts and on very large lakes. Breeds on bodies of fresh water in Arctic tundra.

Local Sites
Distinctive and elegant, the Long-tailed Duck is common on the open waters of Chesapeake Bay from Sandy Point State Park south to Point Lookout State Park—both excellent locations to find it in winter. Try also Ocean City Inlet.

FIELD NOTES The Long-tailed Duck is the only duck that undergoes two complete molts every breeding season, in addition to the molt into its eclipse plumage. As each bird apparently follows its own molting schedule, drakes seen on the same day in the same area may appear quite different from one another.

Breeding | Adult male

BUFFLEHEAD

Bucephala albeola L 13.5" (34 cm)

FIELD MARKS

Small duck with large puffy head, steep forehead, and short bill

Male has large white head patch and a glossy black back

Female is gray-brown overall with small, elongated white patches on either side of her head

Behavior

Often seen in small flocks, some birds keeping a lookout while others dive for aquatic insects, snails, and small fish. Like all diving ducks, its feet are set well back on its body to swiftly propel it through the water. Able to take off directly out of water, unlike many other diving ducks. Monogamous, Buffleheads are believed to stay with the same mate for years and to faithfully return to the same nesting site each season. Both sexes are generally silent away from the breeding grounds.

Habitat

Found on sheltered bays, rivers, and lakes in winter. Breeds primarily in Canada.

Local Sites

Easy locations are Sandy Point State Park, the waterfronts at Cambridge and Chesapeake beaches, and Sinepuxent Bay behind Assateague Island.

FIELD NOTES In its boreal forest breeding grounds in Canada, this smallest of North American diving ducks nests almost exclusively in cavities created by the Northern Flicker (*Colaptes auratus*); a nesting site so tiny that it is speculated to have influenced the Bufflehead's own small size.

Breeding | Adult male

COMMON GOLDENEYE

Bucephala clangula L 18.5" (47 cm)

FIELD MARKS

Head black with greenish tinge on breeding male, brown on female

Male has white patches between eyes and bill; female has white neck ring and gray breast

Male is black above with white scapulars; female grayish above

Behavior

A diving duck, may be seen foraging in flocks, often with much of the flock diving simultaneously for aquatic insects, invertebrates, and plants. With feet located near its tail, this bird is an expert swimmer and diver, but walks very awkwardly on land. Male gives a nasal, descending *keeer* call; female occasionally gives a harsh, croaking *gack*. Listen as well for the low, stirring whistle made by the wings of the adult male in flight.

Habitat

Inhabits deep, open lakes and rivers near woodlands. In winter, also found in coastal areas. Look for this hardy duck even in open water between ice floes.

Local Sites

May be seen on Chesapeake Bay waters in winter, especially the lower Patuxent River. Sandy Point State Park or the Chesapeake Beach waterfront are two other good places to try.

FIELD NOTES Distinctive marks to look for in the field on the female Common Goldeneye (inset) include her brown head, yellowish eye, mostly black bill with a yellowish tip, and her white neck ring. Both sexes show a large amount of white on their wings in flight.

Breeding | Adult male

HOODED MERGANSER

Lophodytes cucullatus L 18" (46 cm)

FIELD MARKS
Puffy, rounded crest

Male's white head patches are fan-shaped and conspicuous; black bill, back, and tail; white breast with two vertical black bars; chestnut sides

Female brownish gray overall with a rusty brown crest

Behavior
Dives expertly, using its wings and feet to propel itself underwater. Serrated bill is good for catching fish; also feeds on crustaceans, insects, and plants. Known at times to hunt cooperatively with other merganser species. Takes flight directly out of water, and moves swiftly with rapid wing beats. Though generally silent, throaty grunts and chatter can sometimes be heard from these ducks. A displaying drake will also emit a froglike growl.

Habitat
Winters on fresh and brackish water. In breeding season, found on woodland ponds, rivers, and backwaters, especially swamps.

Local Sites
Breeders are rare statewide, but wintering groups can be found at lakes and ponds anywhere. Especially good spots are Patuxent Research Refuge, West Ocean City Pond, and Hughes Hollow.

FIELD NOTES A distinctive field mark on the female Hooded Merganser (inset) is her thin, serrated bill with a dark upper mandible and a yellowish lower one. In flight, note both sexes' crests are flattened.

Year-round | Adult male

RED-BREASTED MERGANSER

Mergus serrator L 23" (58 cm)

FIELD MARKS

Male has a dark green head, a streaked breast, and a black back

Female has chestnut head, whitish chin and throat, and a gray-brown back

Both sexes have shaggy double crest and a red bill, hooked at tip

Behavior

Long, thin, serrated bill aids in catching small fish, the Red-breasted's principal food source. Flaps wings and runs across water or land to take off, but once airborne is a strong, swift flyer, attaining speeds near 80 mph. This merganser is a powerful swimmer using its rear-set feet to propel itself underwater. Often silent, the Red-breasted hen may sometimes utter hoarse croaks.

Habitat

Typically winters along the coast, seeking sheltered bays, estuaries, and harbors that provide calm salt water in which to forage.

Local Sites

Most common in coastal bays in winter; try Ocean City or Assateague Island. In migration, widespread on Chesapeake Bay, occurs occasionally on inland lakes.

FIELD NOTES Similar in size and shape to the Red-breasted, the Common Merganser, *Mergus merganser* (inset: male), prefers large freshwater lakes, such as Triadelphia Reservoir, or the Susquehanna River above Conowingo Dam. The Common Merganser's crest is less shaggy.

Year-round | Adult male

WILD TURKEY

Meleagris gallopavo Male L 46" (117 cm) Female L 37" (94 cm)

FIELD MARKS

Large, with purple, green, and bronze iridescent plumage

Unfeathered blue and pink head with red wattles

Male has blackish breast tuft

Female smaller, less iridescent

Behavior
Largest of game birds, the turkey lives communally in small flocks. A ground feeder by day, the Wild Turkey roosts in trees at night. Forages for nuts, seeds, fruit, insects, frogs, and lizards. Flies well for short distances when alarmed, but prefers to walk or run. Females raise large broods, nesting in leaf-lined hollows in brush or woodlands. Male's characteristic display during breeding season involves puffing out his chest, swelling his wattles, spreading his tail, and rattling his wings, all while gobbling and strutting. In spring, the male's gobbling call may be heard from as far as a mile away.

Habitat
Frequents open forests, grainfields, and forest edges.

Local Sites
Increasing numbers of turkeys are found in western Maryland and on the Eastern Shore. Pocomoke State Forest, fields east of Blackwater N. W. R., or fields south of Oakland are especially good bets.

FIELD NOTES The Ruffed Grouse, *Bonasa umbellus* (inset: male gray morph), is generally shy and elusive, except in spring when the male attracts females by raising his crest and neck ruff, fanning his tail and beating his wings rapidly, making a hollow drumming noise as he struts. Found from Frederick County west.

Year-round | Adult male

NORTHERN BOBWHITE

Colinus virginianus L 9.8" (25 cm)

FIELD MARKS

Mottled reddish brown quail
with short gray tail

Throat and eye stripe white in
male, buff-colored in female

Whitish underparts with
black scalloping

Behavior

A ground feeder, the Northern Bobwhite forages for
seeds, grains, insects, and leaf buds. Feeds and roosts in
a covey except during nesting season. Nests on the
ground, usually under a woven cover of pine needles,
grass, and vegetation with an opening on one side.
When alarmed, it is more likely to run than to fly.
Male's call is a rising, whistled *bob-white*, heard chiefly
in late spring and summer. A whistled *hoy* can also be
heard year-round.

Habitat

The Northern Bobwhite has the largest range of all
North American quail. It prefers farmland and open
woodlands with plentiful underbrush.

Local Sites

The Northern Bobwhite has declined drastically in the
last two decades, and is now rare or gone from much
of the region. The best places to try are Blackwater
National Wildlife Refuge or E. A. Vaughn Wildlife
Management Area.

FIELD NOTES To keep warm at night, a covey of Northern Bob-
whites, sometimes as many as 30, will roost on the ground in a
circle, with heads facing outward and tails pushed together so
that their bodies are in contact.

Nonbreeding | Adult

COMMON LOON

Gavia immer L 32" (81 cm)

FIELD MARKS

In winter: dark gray above, pale below; blue-gray bill; dark nape has white indentation each side

In spring and summer: back black-and-white checked; head dark green; neck striped; black bill

Behavior

A diving bird; eats fish up to 10 inches long, which it grasps with its pointed beak. Forages by diving and swimming underwater, propelled by large, paddle-shaped feet. Can stay submerged for up to three minutes at depths down to 250 feet. It is nearly impossible for the Common Loon to walk on land. Generally remains silent on wintering grounds.

Habitat

Winters in coastal waters, or inland on large lakes.

Local Sites

Spring and fall migrants may be seen on Chesapeake Bay or may stop on any large lake. In winter look for the Common Loon at Ocean City or off Point Lookout.

FIELD NOTES The dark red throat patch of the Red-throated Loon, *Gavia stellata* (inset: nonbreeding), is visible only during breeding season. In winter, the Red-throated can be identified by the white on its face, which extends farther back than that on the Common Loon, and by its habit of holding its thinner bill angled slightly upward. It is found mostly on the open ocean in Maryland.

Breeding | Adult

PIED-BILLED GREBE

Podilymbus podiceps L 13.5" (34 cm)

FIELD MARKS
Small and short-necked

Breeding adult brownish gray
overall; black ring around stout,
whitish bill; black chin and throat

Winter birds lose bill ring; chin
becomes white; plumage is
browner overall

Behavior
The most widespread of North American grebes, the
Pied-billed remains for the most part on water, seldom
on land or in flight. Dives for aquatic insects, small fish,
frogs, and vegetable matter. When alarmed, it slowly
sinks, holding only its head above the water's surface.
Like most grebes, the Pied-billed eats its own feathers
and feeds them to its young, perhaps to protect their
stomach linings from fish bones or animal shells. Song
is a series of slightly hollow, rapid-paced *kuh-kuh-kuh*s
or *k'owh-k'owh-k'owh*s.

Habitat
Prefers nesting around freshwater marshes and ponds.
Also found in more open waters of large bays and
rivers. Winters on both fresh and salt water.

Local Sites
Breeds at Deal Island W. M. A. and winters widely, with
Patuxent Research Refuge and Black Hills Reservoir
being good spots for wintering or migrant birds.

FIELD NOTES The black-and-white Horned
Grebe, *Podiceps auritus* (inset: nonbreeding), is a common spring migrant and uncommon
fall migrant on Chesapeake Bay (rarer inland). It
winters commonly on the coast.

Year-round | Adult

WILSON'S STORM-PETREL

Oceanites oceanicus L 7.3" (19 cm) WS 16" (41 cm)

FIELD MARKS
Blackish plumage with brown
upperwing bar

White rump

Long legs; yellow webbing
on feet

Small size

Behavior
Can survive on fish oil alone, but may also pick small
organisms or pieces of food from the water's surface.
Flight fluttery, low to water, reminiscent of a swallow.
May patter feet on water to stir up food; often follows
boat wake. Comes to land only to nest, but it may rest
on the water. May occur singly or in small flocks. May
be active day or night. Generally silent.

Habitat
Pelagic; occurs on open ocean. Nests in burrows on
islands in southern hemisphere, migrating to northern
hemisphere oceans during the northern summer.

Local Sites
Almost never seen from shore, but is a common sight
from April to September for boaters on the open ocean,
three or more miles off Ocean City. Recently found in
Chesapeake Bay between Point Lookout and Smith
Island, and might be seen from the passenger ferry
between those two points.

FIELD NOTES Considered the most abundant bird in the world.
Wilson's Storm-Petrel is a member of the order Procellariiformes,
which also includes albatrosses and shearwaters, all of which
spend their entire lives at sea, except when nesting. Breeding is
almost exclusively on protected islands, where all species lay a
single egg and spend a long time caring for the young.

Breeding | Adult

BROWN PELICAN

Pelecanus occidentalis L 48" (122 cm) WS 84" (213 cm)

FIELD MARKS

Exceptionally long bill with dark gray throat pouch

Silvery gray above; blackish brown below; white crown; pale yellow forehead

Breeding adult's hindneck is chestnut; winter adult's is white

Behavior

Dives from the air into water to capture prey. On impact, its throat pouch balloons open, scooping up small fish. Tilts its bill downward to drain water, tosses its head back to swallow. Sometimes gather in large groups over transitory schools of fish, attracting other seabirds to the feeding frenzy. Flocks travel in long, staggered lines, alternately flapping and gliding in unison. For years endangered, this species is currently making a significant recovery following a severe decline in its population due to pesticide poisoning.

Habitat

Largely coastal, the Brown Pelican makes its home along the shore in sheltered bays and near beaches. Breeds on islands in large stick nests.

Local Sites

Has recently colonized Maryland. Look for it at Ocean City, Point Lookout, or Smith Island.

FIELD NOTES Related to pelicans, the Northern Gannet, *Morus bassanus* (inset: adult), is an oceanic bird that occurs in Maryland in winter. Its pointed head and tail are distinctive. Immatures are overall brown; adults are white with black on the outer half of the wing.

Breeding | Adult

DOUBLE-CRESTED CORMORANT

Phalacrocorax auritus L 32" (81 cm) WS 52" (132 cm)

FIELD MARKS

Black overall; facial skin yellow-orange; pale bill hooked at tip

Distinctive kinked neck in flight

Breeding adult has tufts of black feathers behind eyes

Immature has pale neck and breast

Behavior

In pursuit of prey, the Double-crested can dive to considerable depths, propelling itself with fully webbed feet. Uses its hooked bill to grasp fish. Feeds on a variety of aquatic life. May swim submerged to the neck, bill pointed slightly skyward. When it leaves the water, it perches on a branch, dock, or piling and half-spreads its wings to dry. Soars at times, its neck in an S-shape. Nests near water either in trees or on rocks. Silent for the most part, but sometimes emits a deep grunt.

Habitat

Found along coasts, at inland lakes, and near rivers; it has adapted to fresh and saltwater environments.

Local Sites

From March to November it is common anywhere on Chesapeake Bay or along the coast. In spring and fall it may also be seen at larger lakes and rivers.

FIELD NOTES Much rarer than Double-crested, Great Cormorant, *Phalacrocorax carbo* (inset: adult), is seen in winter at Ocean City and Point Lookout State Park. To tell it from Double-crested, look for adult's white throat and flank patches; immature's dark chest, white belly.

Breeding | Adult

GREAT BLUE HERON

Ardea herodias L 46" (117 cm) WS 72" (183 cm)

FIELD MARKS

Gray-blue overall; white foreneck with black streaks; yellowish bill

Black stripe extends above eye

Breeding adult has plumes on its head, neck, and back

Juvenile has dark crown; no plumes

Behavior

Waits for prey to come into its range, then spears it with a quick thrust of its sharp bill. Eats almost anything, from fish, snakes, and frogs, to mice and woodchucks, to large insects and some small birds. Flies with its head folded back onto its shoulders in an S-curve, typical of other herons as well. When threatened, draws its neck back with plumes erect and points its bill at antagonist. Pairs build stick nests high in trees in loose association with other Great Blue pairs. Mostly silent away from its nest, but sometimes emits an annoyed, deep, guttural *kraaank* as it takes flight.

Habitat

Hunts for aquatic creatures in marshes and swamps, and for small mammals in fields and forest edges.

Local Sites

These birds dwell at lakes, ponds, marshy wetlands, and rivers year-round wherever waters remain ice free.

FIELD NOTES A formidable predator, the Great Blue Heron feeds primarily on fish, but has also been known to eat mammals as large as muskrats and birds as large as Clapper Rails (pages 92-93). Prey is swallowed whole; it will often wet the fur of mammalian prey to devour it more easily. It has been known to choke to death on prey items that are too large.

Breeding | Adult

GREAT EGRET

Ardea alba L 39" (99 cm) WS 51" (130 cm)

FIELD MARKS

Large white heron with heavy yellow bill, black legs and feet

Breeding adult has long plumes trailing from its back, extending beyond the tail

Blue-green lores while breeding

Behavior

Stalks its prey slowly and methodically in shallow water, uses its sharply pointed bill to capture small fish, aquatic insects, frogs, and crayfish. Also known to hunt snakes, birds, and small mammals. Occasionally forages in groups or steals food from smaller birds. Nests in trees or shrubs 10 to 40 feet above the ground. Colonies may have as many as a hundred birds. Generally silent except when nesting or disturbed, when it may emit a guttural *kraak* or repeated *cuk-cuk-cuk* notes.

Habitat

Inhabits both fresh and saltwater wetlands.

Local Sites

Though it breeds in salt marshes and on islands, the Great Egret may wander inland during late summer and fall. Assateague and Smith Islands, Deal Island Wildlife Management Area, and Blackwater National Wildlife Refuge provide reliable summer viewing.

FIELD NOTES Early in the breeding season, the Great Egret grows long, ostentatious feathers called aigrettes from its scapulars. In the late 1800s, aigrettes were so sought after by the millinery industry that Great Egrets were hunted nearly to extinction. The grassroots campaign to end the slaughter later developed into the National Audubon Society. Today, loss of wetlands continues to limit the population of Great Egrets and other herons.

Nonbreeding | Adult

SNOWY EGRET

Egretta thula L 24" (61 cm) WS 41" (104 cm)

FIELD MARKS

White heron with slender black bill and legs; yellow eyes, lores, and feet

Breeding adult has upward-curving plumes on head, neck, and back; nonbreeding adult lacks plumes

Behavior

An active feeder, the Snowy Egret may be seen running in shallows, chasing after its prey of fish, insects, and crustaceans. Also forages by stirring up bottom water with feet to flush out prey. In breeding display, the Snowy Egret raises its plumage, pumps its head up and down, and flashes the skin at the base of its bill, which has turned from yellow to vermilion. Also during breeding season, the generally quiet bird will bray gutturally, pointing its bill straight up.

Habitat

Prefers wetlands and sheltered bays along the coastline. Nests several feet up in trees among mixed colonies including heron, egret, and ibis species.

Local Sites

Look for it in summer at Assateague and Smith Islands, Deal Island Wildlife Management Area, and Black-water National Wildlife Refuge.

FIELD NOTES An Old World species, the Cattle Egret, *Bubulcus ibis,* probably emigrated from Africa in the early 1900s. By the 1970s, it had colonized most of the continental U.S. It is smaller than the Snowy, with a stubbier yellow or orange bill. Breeding (inset), it acquires orange-buff plumes. It is pure white in nonbreeding season.

Nonbreeding | Adult

LITTLE BLUE HERON

Egretta caerulea L 24" (61 cm) WS 40" (102 cm)

FIELD MARKS

Slate blue; dull green legs and feet; blue-gray bill and lores

Adult in high breeding plumage has reddish purple head and neck, black legs and feet

Immature bird white with gray wing tips, grayish bill and lores

Behavior

A slow and methodical feeder, hunts for fish and small crustaceans. Strictly carnivorous, it snags its prey with its sharply pointed bill. Like all herons, the Little Blue may be seen preening its contour and flight feathers with its pectinate, or comblike, middle toes. At colonies, breeding male sings *ee-oo-ah-ee-ee.* Both male and female emit hoarse croaks and squawks.

Habitat

Prefers freshwater ponds, lakes, and marshes, and coastal saltwater wetlands. Both sexes build nest of sticks and twigs low to the ground in a tree or shrub.

Local Sites

Little Blue Herons can be found in summer at Assateague and Smith Islands, Deal Island Wildlife Management Area, and Blackwater National Wildlife Refuge. Immatures are similar to Snowy Egrets (page 66-67), but more likely to turn up away from tidewater, mostly in July and August.

FIELD NOTES The Tricolored Heron, *Egretta tricolor* (inset), is about the same size as the Little Blue, but is set apart by its white foreneck and belly, its long yellowish bill, and its dull yellow legs. It breeds on the lower Chesapeake Bay and along the coast.

Year-round | Adult

GREEN HERON

Butorides virescens L 18" (46 cm) WS 26" (66 cm)

FIELD MARKS

Small, chunky heron with blue-green back and crown, sometimes raised to form shaggy crest

Back and sides of neck deep chestnut, throat white

Short yellow to orange legs

Behavior

Usually a solitary hunter, a Green Heron that lands near one of its kind is likely to be attacked. Stands motionless in or near water, waiting for a fish to come close enough for a swift attack. Spends most of its day in the shade, sometimes perched in trees or shrubs. When alarmed, it may make a show by flicking its tail, raising its crest, and elongating its neck. Both sexes build nest in tree or shrub, generally not far from the ground. A sharp *skeow* may be heard in flight.

Habitat

Found in a variety of wetland habitats but prefers streams, ponds, and marshes with woodland cover.

Local Sites

From April to September the widespread Green Heron can be found at wooded lakes, ponds, and other wetlands. Patuxent Research Refuge and Blackwater National Wildlife Refuge are just two good locales.

FIELD NOTES An innovative hunter, the Green Heron will sometimes, though rarely, stand at the edge of shallow water and toss twigs, insects, even earthworms into the water as lures to attract unsuspecting minnows into its striking range. This is one of the few instances of tool use in the bird world.

Breeding | Adult

BLACK-CROWNED NIGHT-HERON

Nycticorax nycticorax L 25" (64 cm) WS 44" (112 cm)

FIELD MARKS

Black crown and back

Two to three white hindneck plumes, longest when breeding

White underparts and face; gray wings, tail, and sides of neck

Immature streaked brown

Behavior
Primarily a nocturnal feeder. Even when feeding during the day, remains in the shadows, almost motionless, waiting for prey to come within range. Forages for fish, frogs, rodents, reptiles, mollusks, eggs, and nestlings. Black-crowneds, consumers of fairly large prey, are susceptible to accumulating contaminants; their population status is an indicator of environmental quality. Call heard in flight is a gutteral *quok*.

Habitat
Has adapted to a wide range of habitats, including salt marshes, brackish and freshwater wetlands, and lakeshores that provide cover and forage. Nests in colonies high up in trees.

Local Sites
Occurs year-round at West Ocean City Pond, Deal Island Wildlife Management Area, Conowingo Dam, and the National Zoo in Washington, D.C.

FIELD NOTES The adult Yellow-crowned Night-Heron, *Nyctanassa violacea* (inset), is also a nocturnal feeder with long, white neck plumes. A black-and-white head and a largely gray body distinguish the Yellow-crowned from its cousin. It is found at Smith Island and Lake Roland (near Baltimore).

Year-round | Adult

TURKEY VULTURE

Cathartes aura   L 27" (69 cm)   WS 69" (175 cm)

FIELD MARKS

In flight, contrasting two-toned
underwings; long tail extends
beyond feet

Brownish black feathers on body;
silver gray flight feathers

Unfeathered red head; ivory bill;
head and bill black on juvenile

Behavior

An adept flier, the Turkey Vulture soars high above the
ground in search of carrion and refuse. Rocks from
side to side in flight, seldom flapping its wings. Well
developed sense of smell allows the Turkey Vulture to
locate carrion concealed in forest settings. Feeds heavily when food is available but can go days without if
necessary. Nests solitarily in abandoned buildings or
hollow logs and trees. Generally silent, but will emit
soft hisses and grunts while feeding or if threatened.

Habitat

Hunts in open country and woodlands, and in urban
dumps and landfills. Often seen over highways.

Local Sites

Easily seen in the skies regionwide during summer,
Turkey Vultures largely withdraw from the far west
(Garrett County) during winter.

FIELD NOTES The less common Black Vulture,
Coragyps atratus (inset), is not as efficient at
finding a meal, but is more aggressive. It will sometimes follow a Turkey Vulture to its find and claim it
as its own. Look for the Black Vulture's shorter tail
and white restricted to the primaries.

Year-round | Adult

OSPREY

Pandion haliaetus L 22-25" (56-64 cm) WS 58-72" (147-183 cm)

FIELD MARKS

Dark brown above, white below; white head, dark eye stripe; females usually have darker neck streaks

Slightly arched in flight, wings appear bent back or "crooked"

Pale plumage fringing in juvenile

Behavior
Hunts by soaring, hovering, then diving down and plunging feet-first into water, snatching its prey with long, lethal talons. Feeds exclusively on fish. The Osprey's specialized diet makes it susceptible to accumulating contaminants, such as DDT. Nests near bodies of fresh or salt water. Bulky nests are built atop dead trees or on specialized man-made platforms. Call is a series of clear, resonant, whistled *kyew*s.

Habitat
Forages in a variety of aquatic habitats, including lakes, rivers, and reservoirs. Highly migratory, these birds can be found on every continent except Antarctica.

Local Sites
Ospreys take advantage of channel markers as nest sites throughout the Chesapeake Bay and its estuaries. Migrants can be seen in spring and fall at inland lakes or ridges, such as Washington Monument State Park or Town Hill.

FIELD NOTES The use of DDT and other chemical pollutants during the 1950s and 1960s decimated the Osprey population in Maryland. The population has since rebounded and it is once again common. Bald Eagles (next page), and Peregrine Falcons (pages 90-91) have enjoyed similar success stories.

Year-round | Adult

BALD EAGLE

Haliaeetus leucocephalus L 31-37" (79-94 cm) WS 70-90" (178-229 cm)

FIELD MARKS

Distinctive white head and tail

Large yellow beak, feet, and eyes

Brown body

Juveniles mostly dark, showing
blotchy white on underwing
and tail

Behavior

The national bird of the United States. A rock-steady
flier, the Bald Eagle rarely swerves or tips on its flattened wings. Feeds mainly on fish, but sometimes on
waterfowl, carrion, or small mammals. Often steals fish
from other birds of prey. Bald Eagles lock talons and
cartwheel together through the sky in an elaborate
courtship dance. Nests solitarily in tall trees or on cliffs.
Call is a weak, almost inaudible *kak-kak-kak*.

Habitat

This member of the sea-eagle group generally lives and
feeds along seacoasts or along rivers and lakes.

Local Sites

Chesapeake Bay hosts the largest East Coast population
north of Florida. Blackwater National Wildlife Refuge
is unrivaled as a place to see the Bald Eagle well; in
winter roosts of 100 or more congregate in the area.

FIELD NOTES An immature Bald Eagle (inset:
second year) shows a variable amount of white
spotting on its head, breast, and underwings. It
is not until its fifth year that it acquires the
characteristic stark white head of the adult.

Year-round | Adult male

NORTHERN HARRIER

Circus cyaneus L 17-23" (43-58 cm) WS 38-48" (97-122 cm)

FIELD MARKS

Adult male grayish above, white below; female brown, white below with brown streaks

Slim body; long, narrow wings

Long tail with white on the rump

Juvenile cinnamon brown below

Behavior

Generally perches low and flies close to the ground, wings upraised, searching for birds, mice, frogs, and other prey. Seldom soars high except during migration and in an exuberant, acrobatic courtship display, when the male loops and somersaults in the air. Often found hunting in the dim light of dawn or dusk. During winter, roosts communally on the ground. Nests on the ground. At breeding site gives a thin, insistent whistle or a high-pitched *kek-kek-kek.*

Habitat

Once called the Marsh Hawk, the Northern Harrier frequents grassy wetlands and open fields.

Local Sites

Very local breeders, mostly in salt marshes such as those at Deal Island Wildlife Management Area. In migration and winter they are more widespread, but still most common at extensive salt marshes. Assateague and Elliott Islands are also likely areas.

FIELD NOTES A Northern Harrier gliding high overhead can look like a falcon, due to its long, broad tail. Look for the bright white on its rump, one of the most noticeable field marks of any of the hawk species.

Juvenile

COOPER'S HAWK

Accipiter cooperii L 14-20" (36-51 cm) WS 29-37" (74-94 cm)

FIELD MARKS

Blue-gray upperparts; reddish
bars across breast, belly

Dark gray cap; bright red eyes

Long, rounded, barred tail with
white terminal band

Juvenile brown with yellow eyes

Behavior

Scans for prey from a perch, then attacks with a sudden
burst of speed. Also scans for prey while soaring. Flies
fast and close to the ground, using brush to conceal its
rapid attack. Typically feeds on birds, rabbits, rodents,
reptiles, and insects. Known to hold prey underwater to
drown it. Gives a high *kew-kew-kew* call at nest site.

Habitat

Prefers broken, especially deciduous, woodlands and
streamside groves. Has adapted to fragmented woodlands created by urban and suburban development.

Local Sites

May be encountered regionwide in any season. Most
common in winter, when it may hunt at backyard
feeders. Migrants can be observed at the coast or at
ridge-top sites like Washington Monument park.

FIELD NOTES Distinguishing a Cooper's from a Sharp-
shinned Hawk, *Accipiter striatus* (inset: juvenile, left;
adult, right), is one of birding's more difficult identifica-
tions. Both species are largely brown as juveniles;
blue-gray above, barred rufous below as adults.
The Sharp-shinned is slightly smaller, has a
squared-off tail, and its neck does not extend as
far out in flight. It is more common in the region in
migration and winter, but largely absent in summer.

Year-round | Adult

RED-SHOULDERED HAWK

Buteo lineatus L 15-19" (38-48 cm) WS 37-42" (94-107 cm)

FIELD MARKS

Adult has reddish shoulders and wing linings; pale spotting above

Breast barred reddish with dark streaks; head has a grayish cast

In flight, shows black tail with white bands and a pale crescent at base of primaries

Behavior

Flies with several wing beats, followed by a glide on flattened wings. Look for it during fall migration, saving its energy by soaring on rising currents of warm air, called thermals. Hunts from low perches for snakes, amphibians, small mammals, and an occasional small bird. Nests close to tree trunks, 10 to 200 feet up. Returns to the same territory for years, sometimes even passing nests along to succeeding generations. Call is an evenly spaced series of clear, high *KEE-ahh* notes.

Habitat

Prefers woodlands, especially moist, mixed woods near water and swamps.

Local Sites

Breeds in forests and woodlands, even in urban and suburban areas across the state. Look for them along the Pocomoke River. Often seen on roadside signs in the Baltimore/Washington, D.C. corridor.

FIELD NOTES The Broad-winged Hawk, *Buteo platypterus* (inset: adult), is an uncommon breeder but a common migrant. Large flocks fly over the Piedmont and western ridges in mid-September. Look for its dark-bordered white underwings and black and white tail bands.

Year-round | Adult

RED-TAILED HAWK

Buteo jamaicensis L 22" (56 cm) WS 50" (127 cm)

FIELD MARKS

Brown above; red tail on adults

Whitish belly with broad band of dark streaking

Dark bar on leading edge of underwing

Immature has brown, banded tail

Behavior

Watch for the Red-tailed Hawk circling above, searching for rodents, sometimes kiting, or hanging motionless on the wind. Uses thermals to gain lift and limit its energy expenditure while soaring. Perches for long intervals on telephone poles and other man-made structures, often in urban areas. Nests in large trees, on cliffs, or on man-made structures; often uses old nests abandoned by other hawks. Listen for its distinctive call, a harsh, rising then descending *shee-eeee-arrr.*

Habitat

Found in a variety of habitats from woods to prairies to farmland, and even in urban settings. Common at habitat edges, where field meets forest or wetlands meet woodlands, favored for the variety of prey found there.

Local Sites

The region's most common resident hawk is conspicuous at all seasons when perched along roadsides and circling above highways throughout the state.

FIELD NOTES While perched, Red-taileds are easy to spot, but when migrating, the hawks soar at altitudes up to 5,000 feet, appearing as nothing more than specks in the sky.

Year-round | Adult male

AMERICAN KESTREL

Falco sparverius L 10.5" (27 cm) WS 23" (58 cm)

FIELD MARKS

Russet back and tail; streaked
tawny to pale underparts

Two black stripes on white face

Male has blue-gray wing coverts

Female has russet wing coverts
and russet streaks on her breast

Behavior

Feeds on insects, reptiles, mice, and other small
mammals. Hovers over prey, then plunges down for the
kill. Will also feed on small birds, especially in winter.
Regularly seen perched on fences and telephone lines,
bobbing its tail with frequency. Nests in tree holes,
barns, or man-made boxes using little or no nesting
material. Has clear, shrill call of *killy-killy-killy* or *klee-
klee-klee,* given year-round.

Habitat

North America's most widely distributed falcon, found
in open country and in cities, often mousing along
highway medians or sweeping along riparian areas.

Local Sites

Declining severely in numbers, the American Kestrel is
now a rare breeder regionwide. It is more common in
winter, and most common as a migrant at such places as
Washington Monument State Park or Assateague Island.

FIELD NOTES The kestrel population of Maryland is threatened by
factors such as competition for nesting holes with the introduced
European Starling (*Sturnus vulgaris*), and an increasing amount
of farmland being given over to forest.

Immature

PEREGRINE FALCON

Falco peregrinus L 16-20" (41-51 cm) WS 36-44" (91-112 cm)

FIELD MARKS

Blue-black crown and nape

Black extends below eye, forming distinctive "helmet"

Adult shows rufous wash below

Juvenile is brownish above; underparts heavily streaked

Behavior

This incredibly fast raptor hunts by flying high on powerful wingbeats, then swooping in on prey in a spectacular dive that can clock in at 175 mph or more. Also flies low over water to surprise waterfowl prey. Feeds primarily on birds, the larger of which may be knocked out of the air and subsequently eaten on the ground. Nests on cliffs, bridges, or tall buildings in cities with very little nesting material. Though usually silent, gives out loud *kak-kak-kak* call at nesting area.

Habitat

Traditionally breeds near cliffs; but now also established in cities. Hunts a wide area and in a variety of habitats.

Local Sites

Downtown Baltimore and the marsh towers at Deal Island W. M. A. are well-known breeding areas. In October watch for migrants hunting the dunes on Assateague Island.

FIELD NOTES The Merlin, *Falco columbarius* (inset: male, left; female, right), is another fast, powerful, and aggressive falcon that visits the region, primarily on migration and mostly along the coast. It is smaller than the Peregrine and lacks the Peregrine's distinctive "helmet."

Year-round | Adult

CLAPPER RAIL

Rallus longirostris **L** 14.5" (37 cm)

FIELD MARKS
Grayish edges on brown-centered back feathers; olive wing coverts

Gray-brown flanks with white bars

Short tail; broad wings

Long, thin, slightly decurved bill

Grayish cheeks

Behavior
This secretive bird usually remains concealed in marsh vegetation. Uses long, thin bill to probe into crevices and holes, such as those of fiddler crabs, worms, and other crustaceans, located under the surface of shallow water. Bobs its head and flicks its tail as it walks. Its distinctive call is an accelerating, then slowing, crescendo of ten or more *kek kek kek* notes, uttered year-round. Also gives an explosive, low-pitched grunting call.

Habitat
Common in coastal salt marshes. Nests are deeply concealed and constructed of marsh vegetation.

Local Sites
Exclusively coastal, Clapper Rails inhabit salt marshes along the Atlantic Coast and the shoreline of lower Chesapeake Bay. Although secretive, they may be seen at low tide along marsh edges and canals at Smith Island or Deal Island W. M. A.

FIELD NOTES The Virginia Rail, *Rallus limicola* (inset: adult), inhabits both fresh and saltwater marshes. Half the Clapper's size and richer colored, its ticking call and high, pig-like grunts can be heard in spring at Elliott Island.

Year-round | Adult

AMERICAN COOT

Fulica americana L 15.5" (39 cm)

FIELD MARKS

Blackish head; slate gray body

Small, reddish brown forehead shield; reddish eyes on adult

Whitish bill with dark band at tip; greenish legs with lobed toes

Juvenile paler with darker bill

Behavior

The coot's distinctive toes are flexible and lobed, permitting it to swim well and to dive for aquatic vegetation and invertebrates. Runs on water, flapping wings rapidly to gain momentum to take flight. Bobs its small head back and forth when walking or swimming. Forages in large flocks, especially during winter. Makes a floating nest anchored to aquatic vegetation. Has a wide vocabulary of grunts, cackles, and chatter.

Habitat

Breeds in freshwater marshes or on lakes and ponds. Winters on both fresh and salt water. The coot has also adapted to human-altered habitats, including sewage lagoons for foraging and suburban lawns for roosting.

Local Sites

The American Coot may be found at lakes and ponds regionwide in migration. Winter flocks gather at such places as Loch Raven Reservoir, Piscataway Creek, and West Ocean City Pond.

FIELD NOTES The Common Moorhen, *Gallinula chloropus* (inset: adult), inhabits many of the same freshwater wetlands as the coot but is much less common. It has a bright red forehead shield which extends onto a red bill tipped with yellow.

Breeding | Adult

BLACK-BELLIED PLOVER

Pluvialis squatarola L 11.5" (29 cm)

FIELD MARKS
Roundish head and body; large
eyes; short black bill; dark legs

Mottled gray; white underparts in
winter and juveniles

Breeding male has frosted cap;
black and white spots on back
and wings; black face and breast

Behavior
Hunts in small, loose groups for invertebrates such
as mollusks, worms, shrimp, insects, and small crabs,
along with eggs and sometimes berries. Locates prey
by sight, runs across the ground, stops, then runs off
again. In this respect, a plover has a similar hunting
style to that of a thrush, such as an American Robin.
Long, pointed wings enable swift flight. Listen for the
Black-bellied Plover's drawn-out three-note whistle,
pee-oo-ee, the second note lower in pitch.

Habitat
This shorebird prefers sandy beaches, mudflats, and
salt marshes. Rarely found in interior regions. Breeds
on the Arctic tundra.

Local Sites
Reliably found only along the immediate coast, seek the
Black-bellied on mudflats and beaches at Ocean City
(4th Street, bayside) or Assateague Island.

FIELD NOTES During spring migration, look
for the Black-bellied's characteristic breeding
plumage (opposite). During winter though, the
Black-bellied sheds its contrasting black and
white feathers and dons a drabber gray plumage
(inset) to blend into its sandy environs.

Breeding | Adult female and downy young

PIPING PLOVER

Charadrius melodus L 7.2" (18 cm)

FIELD MARKS

Pale sandy upperparts

White collar; breeding male has variably complete black collar

Orange legs

Stubby bill: orange at base in summer, black in winter

Behavior

Feeds on worms and other invertebrates in the same manner as other plovers: running, stoppping, picking, and then running again. Forages on beaches or mudflats during low tide, roosts in dunes during high tide where its coloration is protective. May perform distraction displays similar to those of the Killdeer (next page) when predators approach its nest, which is a depression in the sand. Fairly vocal, its call is a plaintive *peep* or *peep-lo* for which it is named.

Habitat

Sandy beaches.

Local Sites

There is only a single site to find this endangered species in the region, and it requires a hike of two miles or more. Park at the northernmost parking lot at Assateague Island and walk north toward the northern tip. Piping Plovers nest in the dunes and feed on flats on the bayside and sometimes along the open beach.

FIELD NOTES Although it does not breed in the region, the Semipalmated Plover, *Charadrius semipalmatus* (inset: breeding male), during its migrations is far more common than the Piping. Look for it at any location good for shorebirds; its dark brown back distinguishes it from the Piping.

Year-round | Adult

KILLDEER

Charadrius vociferus L 10.5" (27 cm)

FIELD MARKS

Gray-brown above; white neck and belly; two black breast bands

Black stripe on forehead and one extending back from black bill

Red-orange rump visible in flight

Red orbital ring

Behavior

Often seen running, then stopping on a dime with an inquisitive look, then suddenly jabbing at the ground with its bill. Feeds mainly on insects that live in short vegetation. May gather in loose flocks, but more often seen by itself. Builds its nest on about any spot of open ground, even in residential areas. Listen for the Killdeer's loud, piercing, eponymous call of *kill-dee* or its rising *dee-dee-dee*. Also gives a long, trilled *trrrrrrr* during courtship display or when its nest is threatened by a predator.

Habitat

Although a type of plover—one of the shorebirds—the Killdeer prefers inland grassy regions, but may also be found on shores.

Local Sites

Noisy and active, the abundant Killdeer is easy to find in fields, pastures, golf courses, urban parks, and at the edges of lakes and ponds.

FIELD NOTES If its nest is threatened by an intruder, the Killdeer is known to feign a broken wing, limping to one side, dragging its wing, and spreading its tail in an attempt to lure the threat away from its young. Once the predator is far enough away from the nest, the instantly "healed" Killdeer takes flight.

Year-round | Adult

AMERICAN OYSTERCATCHER

Haematopus palliatus L 18.5" (47 cm)

FIELD MARKS

Large, red-orange bill; pink legs

Black head and neck; dark brown back and tail

White underparts and wing stripe

Juvenile is scaly-looking above, with dark tip on bill

Behavior
Feeds in shallow water alone or in a flock. It uses its chisel-shaped bill to crack an opening in the shells of clams, oysters, and mussels; it then severs the shellfish's constrictor muscle and pries the shell open. Also probes sand and mud for worms and crabs. Courtship consists of calls coupled with ritualized flights of shallow, rapid wing beats and displays of side-by-side running or rotating in place. Calls are vocal and variable, including a piercing, repeated whistle; a loud, piping *queep;* and a single loud whistle.

Habitat
Coastal beaches, mudflats, and rocky outcroppings. Nests in a bowl-shaped depression in sand or grass, or on gravel and shells piled above the tide line.

Local Sites
Restricted to the Atlantic Coast and certain islands in the lower Chesapeake Bay, oystercatchers are best found at Ocean City (4th Street, bayside) or Assateague Island.

FIELD NOTES The American Oystercatcher has expanded its range northward. As recently as 1958, oystercatchers were rare in the region.

Nonbreeding | Adult

GREATER YELLOWLEGS

Tringa melanoleuca L 14" (36 cm)

FIELD MARKS
Long, dark, slightly upturned bill;
long, bright yellow-orange legs

Head and neck streaked gray-
brown; white-speckled, gray-
brown back

In breeding season: white underparts barred gray-brown on flanks

Behavior
A forager of snails, crabs, and shrimp; also skims surface of water for insects and larvae. Sprints short distances in pursuit of small fish. Usually seen alone or in small groups, this wary bird sounds an alarm when a hawk or falcon approaches. Call is distinctive series of three or more loud, repeated, descending *tew-tew-tew* notes, heard most often in flight.

Habitat
In migration, frequents a full range of wetlands, including marshes, ponds, lakes, rivers, and reservoirs. Breeds across the Canadian boreal zone.

Local Sites
Found in migration at mud flats, marshes, and wet fields anywhere in the region. Occasionally occurs in winter as well at Blackwater National Wildlife Refuge and Deal Island Wildlife Management Area.

FIELD NOTES The Lesser Yellowlegs, *Tringa flavipes,* is a closely related and almost identically plumaged shorebird. Distinguished by its shorter, straighter bill—about the length of its head—it is smaller in stature and less wary in behavior. The Lesser's call is higher and shorter, consisting of one or two *tew* notes. Look for it at the same locations as the Greater, even side-by-side if you are lucky. Does not winter regularly in the region.

Breeding | Adult

WILLET

Catoptrophorus semipalmatus L 15" (38 cm)

FIELD MARKS

Large, plump, with long gray legs

Breeding adult is heavily mottled; white belly

Winter plumage pale gray above

In flight, shows bold black and white wing pattern

Behavior
The Willet, like other shorebirds, wades in search of prey, probing through mud with its long bill. Feeds primarily on aquatic insects and their larvae. While generally protective as parents, Willets are known to leave unhatched eggs behind once the first young leave the nest. Its breeding call of *pill-will-willet* is the origin of its name; it may also be heard giving a *kip-kip-kip* alarm call.

Habitat
Nests in a variety of coastal wetlands during spring and summer months, sometimes within 200 feet of another Willet nest. Moves south in winter.

Local Sites
An abundant breeder in Maryland salt marshes, Willets are noisy and conspicuous at Elliott Island, Assateague Island, and Deal Island Wildlife Management Area.

FIELD NOTES During courtship displays, the Willet will show its black-and-white wing bands, its most distinctive field mark. Keep an eye out as well for the Willet's white rump.

Breeding | Adult

SPOTTED SANDPIPER

Actitis macularius L 7.5" (19 cm)

FIELD MARKS

Olive-brown upperparts, barred during breeding season

White underparts, spotted brown while breeding

Short, straight orange bill tipped in black; short white wing stripe in flight

Behavior
Often seen singly, feeding on insects, crustaceans, and other invertebrates by plucking them from the water's surface or snatching them from the air. Walks with a constant teetering motion. Flies with stiff, shallow wingbeats. The slightly larger female is the first to establish territory and to defend it during breeding season. Nests in grass near water. Calls include a shrill *peet-weet* and a series of *weet* notes, given in flight.

Habitat
Inhabits sheltered ponds, lakes, streams, and marshes.

Local Sites
Uncommon as a breeder but common as a migrant regionwide. Point Lookout and Sandy Point State Parks and Blackwater National Wildlife Refuge are all fine places to encounter migrant Spotted Sandpipers.

FIELD NOTES Another regular migrant throughout the region, the Solitary Sandpiper, *Tringa solitaria* (inset: breeding), has a longer neck than the Spotted; its lower throat, breast, and sides are streaked blackish brown; its brown upperparts are heavily spotted buffy white; and it has a bold white eye ring. Its call is higher pitched and more emphatic.

Molting | Adult

SANDERLING

Calidris alba L 8" (20 cm)

FIELD MARKS

Winter adult pale gray above, white below

Bill and legs black

Prominent white wing stripe and black leading edge show in flight

Juveniles black and white above

Behavior

Feeds on sandy beaches, chasing retreating waves in order to snatch up newly exposed crustaceans and mollusks, then darting to avoid oncoming surf. Like many shorebirds, may be seen standing for a long time on one leg. Flies swiftly, aided by ample wing length and sharp, pointed wings. Flocks wheel and turn together in the air. Call is a sharp *kip*, often emitted in a series.

Habitat

Winters on sandy beaches of the United States and throughout most of the Southern Hemisphere. Migrates sometimes as many as 8,000 miles from breeding grounds in remote Arctic and subarctic.

Local Sites

Common on sandy beaches of Assateague Island during the entire year (except June). Look for a Sanderling beginning to acquire a rusty wash on its head and back before departing for breeding grounds in early May.

FIELD NOTES The Dunlin, *Calidris alpina* (inset: nonbreeding), is also a small, pale wintering shorebird found on the region's coast, but the Dunlin prefers mudflats to sandy beaches. It is slightly darker above than the Sanderling and has a diffuse, dark gray breast band.

Nonbreeding | Adult

LEAST SANDPIPER

Calidris minutilla L 6" (15 cm)

FIELD MARKS
Short, thin, slightly decurved bill

Gray-brown upperparts

Streaked gray-brown breast band

White belly and undertail coverts

Yellowish to greenish legs

Behavior
Forages for food with its short, spiky bill. Feeds on worms, insects, mollusks, small crabs, and fish, in muddy, sandy, or shallow water. Not wary of humans, it will investigate picnic sites on beaches. If flushed, flies off rapidly in a zigzag flight pattern. The Least Sandpiper's call is a high *kree* or *jeet*.

Habitat
Found in tidal coastal regions and wetlands with exposed mud or sand. Breeds in the Arctic.

Local Sites
Primarily a migrant in the region, the Least Sandpiper frequents mudflats, pond edges, and marshes such as those found at Blackwater National Wildlife Refuge. May and August through September are peak migration times.

FIELD NOTES The most diminutive of shorebirds collectively known as "peeps," the Least Sandpiper's yellow-green legs set it apart from the slightly larger Semipalmated Sandpiper, *Calidris pusilla,* which has black legs. The Least's bill is also slightly downcurved—the Semipalmated's is straight—and its breast band is more pronounced. These two peeps are found at similar sites in Maryland and D.C.

Nonbreeding | Adult

PURPLE SANDPIPER

Calidris maritima L 9" (23 cm)

FIELD MARKS

Upperparts dull blue-gray overall

Underparts whitish with blue-gray streaking

Legs and base of bill orange

Reddish back feathering in summer

Behavior

Forages in small flocks along rocky shorelines, where it probes the intertidal zone for invertebrates. Often associates with Ruddy Turnstones and Sanderlings (pages 110-111). Due to the state's naturally sandy shores, it may not have wintered regularly in Maryland until stone jetties were built in the early 1900s. Call is a harsh *crech*.

Habitat

Rocky shorelines of the North Atlantic. Breeds in the high Arctic.

Local Sites

Purple Sandpipers are reliably seen only on the jetties on either side of Ocean City Inlet. Look for them from December to early May. They are often quite confiding and can be seen at very close range.

FIELD NOTES One of the most strikingly patterned shorebirds, the Ruddy Turnstone, *Arenaria interpres* (inset: breeding), winters with Purple Sandpipers at Ocean City Inlet. Their winter plumage is dull, but by April they acquire their bright breeding plumage.

Year-round | Adult

AMERICAN WOODCOCK

Scolopax minor L 11" (28 cm)

FIELD MARKS
Chunky; mottled brown and gray
above and orange-brown below

Long, stout bill

Short neck, legs, and tail

Large eyes set high in the head

Rounded wings

Behavior
This secretive bird is most often spotted at dusk. It uses
its long bill to probe deep into the damp earth of the
forest floor for its favorite meal of earthworms. Also
eats millipedes, beetles, and flies. Its flexible upper bill
tip allows it to snatch prey below ground. If flushed, it
will fly up abruptly, its wings making a loud, twittering
sound. Its nasal *peent* is heard mainly in spring.

Habitat
Although a shorebird, the American Woodcock prefers
moist woodlands, where it nests on the forest floor.

Local Sites
While one may chance upon a woodcock almost any season, they are best sought on spring evenings when they
call and display in clearings and wood edges. Hughes
Hollow is one place with ample habitat.

FIELD NOTES The slightly smaller Wilson's Snipe,
Gallinago delicata (inset), has a long bill for
probing the mud of wetlands. It has a boldly
striped head and barred flanks. In swooping
display flights, its vibrating outer tail
feathers make quavering hoots.

Breeding | Adult

LAUGHING GULL

Larus atricilla L 16.5" (42 cm) WS 40" (102 cm)

FIELD MARKS

Breeding adult has black hood; white underparts; slate gray wings with black outer primaries

White crescent marks above and below eyes; drooping red bill

In winter, gray wash on head, nape, and neck; black bill

Behavior

Forages for crabs, insects, decayed fish, garbage, and anything else it can get, sometimes plunging its head underwater or harassing beachgoers for popcorn or french fries. In spring, large flocks of Laughing Gulls can be observed feeding on deposits of horseshoe-crab eggs in wet sand. Name comes from characteristic call, *ha-ha-ha-ha*, given when feeding or courting.

Habitat

Common and conspicuous along coastal regions, especially sandy beaches. Nests of grass and aquatic plants are found in marshes or on sand.

Local Sites

Almost impossible to miss at Assateague Island in summer, and is common throughout Chesapeake Bay and up the Potomac River to D.C.

FIELD NOTES It takes three years for the Laughing Gull to attain full adult plumage. The juvenile is brown with a white throat and belly. By the first winter (inset), it still has brown wings, but its sides and back are gray. By the second winter it has lost all brown. Not until the third summer does it develop a black hood, the sign of a full breeding adult.

Nonbreeding | Adult

RING-BILLED GULL

Larus delawarensis L 17.5" (44 cm) WS 48" (122 cm)

FIELD MARKS

Yellow bill with black subterminal ring; pale eye with dark orbital ring

Pale gray upperparts; white underparts; yellowish legs; black primaries show white spots

Head streaked light brown in winter

Behavior
This opportunistic feeder will scavenge for garbage, grains, dead fish, fruit, and marine invertebrates. A vocal gull, it calls, croaks, and cries incessantly, especially during feeding. The call consists of a series of laughing croaks that begins with a short, gruff note and falls into a series of *kheeyaahhh* sounds.

Habitat
Common along shorelines in winter, but also a regular visitor to most inland bodies of water, especially reservoirs in urban areas.

Local Sites
The most likely gull to be found inland, the Ring-billed is common regionwide. Look for it seeking handouts at the National Mall in D.C. or amassing in the thousands at Conowingo Dam or local landfills.

FIELD NOTES The Ring-billed takes three years to reach adult plumage. The first winter (inset) has a gray back, brown wings with dark primaries, and a dark-tipped tail. In its second winter, it looks like an adult with a broader band on its bill, more black on its primaries, blackish spots on the tip of its tail.

Breeding | Adult

HERRING GULL

Larus argentatus L 25" (64 cm) WS 58" (147 cm)

FIELD MARKS
Yellow bill with red mark near tip
of lower mandible

Pale gray mantle in adult

White head and neck streaked
with brown in winter

Pinkish legs and feet

Behavior
Like other gulls, the Herring Gull forages on land and
in sea for shellfish, dead fish, and marine invertebrates.
Flocks congregate where food is abundant, such as at
garbage dumps, near boardwalks, in parking lots, or
around fishing boats. An aggressive forager, the Herring
is known to steal lunches from other birds. Various
calls include *cleew cleew, kyow,* and *kee-oo kee-oo.*
Alarm call is a quick *kek kek kek.*

Habitat
Primarily a coastal bird, the Herring Gull is numerous
along the coast, and less common but still widespread
inland. Generally nests on the ground, but will move
to trees or rooftops if pressed.

Local Sites
Widespread throughout the tidal Chesapeake and
Atlantic Ocean waters. It wanders inland to the Pied-
mont, rarely farther west.

FIELD NOTES Along with several other gull species, the Herring
Gull has benefited from the wasteful habits of humans. Landfills
and offal from fishing boats have greatly increased the food
available for these scavengers, and as a result the Herring Gull
population has increased drastically and the species has
expanded its breeding range well south of its historical limits.

Year-round | Adult

GREAT BLACK-BACKED GULL

Larus marinus L 30" (76 cm) WS 65" (165 cm)

FIELD MARKS

Large gull; adult has large yellow bill with red spot on lower mandible

Black mantle and upper wing; white head, neck, and underparts

White primary tips, tail, and uppertail coverts; pink legs

Behavior

The largest gull in the world, the Great Black-backed will bully smaller gulls and take their lunches. Also scavenges on beaches for mollusks, crustaceans, insects, and eggs; wades in water for fish, roots through garbage for carrion and refuse, and even kills birds as large as cormorants. On breeding grounds, listen for a low, slow *keeeeyaaaahh*.

Habitat

Coastal areas of eastern North America and large inland lakes and rivers. Breeding range is extending southward along the Atlantic coast.

Local Sites

A Great Black-backed gull will occasionally wander into the Piedmont; but they are hard to miss in any season at Sandy Point State Park or Ocean City Inlet.

FIELD NOTES The Lesser Black-backed Gull, *Larus fuscus* (inset: nonbreeding), is actually dark gray on its back and wings and resembles the Herring Gull (previous page), but is darker above and has yellow legs. A recent colonist from Europe, small numbers are now found regularly around Chesapeake Bay, especially at landfills with other gulls.

Breeding | Adult

ROYAL TERN

Sterna maxima L 20" (51 cm) WS 41" (104 cm)

FIELD MARKS

Full black cap acquired briefly, early in breeding season

White crown with black on nape for rest of year

White below, pale gray mantle

Orange-red bill; tail deeply forked

Behavior

Hovers, then plunge-dives 40 to 60 feet into water after prey of fish, shrimp, and crustaceans. Roosts along with other species of terns and gulls on sandbars, beaches, or mudflats. Small groups may cooperate in finding prey; once a school of fish is found, the entire group will soon congregate at that location. Calls in the Royal Tern's large vocabulary include a bleating *kee-rer* and a whistled *tourree*. Juvenile emits a thin *see see see*.

Habitat

Prefers open salt water along coastlines, especially bays and inlets. Nests in dense, mixed colonies with other tern species on sandbars and small, sandy islands.

Local Sites

A very visible colony can be seen on the sandy island in Assawoman Bay, best viewed from 4th Street in Ocean City. It also visits Chesapeake Bay from April to October.

FIELD NOTES The slightly larger Caspian Tern, *Sterna caspia* (inset; breeding), is not as sociable as the Royal Tern and will eat the eggs and young of other tern species. Its bill is thicker and deeper red, the tips of its primaries are duskier, and its tail is not as deeply forked as the Royal's.

Nonbreeding | Adult

FORSTER'S TERN

Sterna forsteri L 14.5" (37 cm)

FIELD MARKS

Pale gray above; white below

Full black cap on breeding adult; only around eye in fall and winter

Orange-red bill with dark tip while breeding; all dark in winter

Long, deeply forked gray tail

Behavior
When feeding, the Forster's flies back and forth over the water, then plunge-dives to capture small fish. May also forage on insects, grabbing them in the air or from the water's surface. Often feeds and flocks with other species of tern. Gives a one-note call, a hoarse, descending *kyarr,* while feeding over water or during breeding season. Also emits a piercing *kit-kit-kit* cry.

Habitat
Winters mainly along coastlines, but also inhabits inland marshes and lakes where abundant fish and insects may be found. Nests in loose colonies in salt marshes atop a platform of grass, or in sand or mud.

Local Sites
Common from April to November, Forster's Tern is easily found at Hains Point in D.C., Point Lookout State Park and Ocean City in Maryland.

FIELD NOTES Compare Forster's Tern to the Common Tern, *Sterna hirundo* (inset: breeding). Forster's Tern is longer-legged and whiter on its wings. In breeding plumage, the Common is grayer on its breast, while only Forster's has the black eye patch in nonbreeding plumage (opposite).

Breeding | Adults

LEAST TERN

Sterna antillarum L 9" (23 cm) WS 20" (51 cm)

FIELD MARKS
Small size

Pale gray upperparts;
white underparts

Black cap with white blaze
on forehead

Breeding: bill and legs yelllow

Behavior
Nests in small colonies where the adults aggressively
protect the nests and young by swooping upon an
intruder, sometimes striking the head with their bills.
Fishes for small minnows in waters near the colony and
brings to the young. Also engages in courtship feeding,
whereby the male ceremoniously feeds the female a
small fish. Calls are a harsh *chir-ee-eep* and intermittent
sharp *kip* notes.

Habitat
Nests on sandy beaches, gravel bars, and sometimes
gravel rooftops near water. Forages primarily in salt or
brackish water, but occasionally in freshwater ponds.

Local Sites
Least Terns nest on islands near Ocean City, but are
increasing locally as nesters on rooftops. Kent Island
and Cambridge support healthy rooftop colonies. It has
even nested atop urban D.C.'s Kennedy Center.

FIELD NOTES Along with the Piping Plover (pages 98-99), the
Least Tern is a beach-nesting species that has run into conflict
with man: in particular, off-road vehicles and unleashed dogs.
Colonies of both bird species are now monitored and protected,
but populations of both species are still considered to be feder-
ally endangered.

Breeding | Adult

BLACK SKIMMER

Rynchops niger L 18" (46 cm) WS 44" (112 cm)

FIELD MARKS

Long, red, black-tipped bill with lower mandible longer than upper

Black back and crown; white face and underparts; red legs

Winter adults show white collar

Female distinctly smaller

Behavior
Uses long, pointed wings to glide low over water while dropping its lower mandible to skim the surface for small fish. Once its bill touches a fish, the maxilla, or upper bill, snaps down to catch prey. Breeds in colonies on beaches, often sharing a site with tern species to take advantage of their aggressive defensive tactics. Makes a yelping bark in nesting colonies or in response to a threat. Pairs sometimes sing a *kow-kow* call together.

Habitat
Prefers sheltered bays, estuaries, coastal marshes, and sometimes inland lakes. Nests very locally in large colonies on barrier islands and salt marshes.

Local Sites
The only reliable place to find skimmers in the region is at Ocean City, particularly the bayside island viewed from 4th Street, known to birders as Skimmer Island.

FIELD NOTES The Black Skimmer has a unique bill: As a feeding adaptation, the lower mandible is considerably longer than the upper. It also has an adaptive pupil, able to contract to a narrow, vertical slit. This capability is thought to protect the eye from bright sunlight glaring off the water's surface.

Year-round | Adult

ROCK PIGEON

Columba livia L 12.5" (32 cm)

FIELD MARKS

Variably plumaged, with head and
neck usually darker than back

White cere at base of dark bill,
pink legs

Iridescent feathers on neck reflect
green, bronze, and purple

Behavior

Feeds on grain, seeds, fruit, and refuse; a frequent
visitor to farms and backyard feeding stations. As it
forages, moves with a short-stepped, "pigeon-toed" gait
while its head bobs back and forth. Courtship display
consists of male puffing out neck feathers, fanning tail,
and turning in circles while cooing. Nests and roosts
primarily on high window ledges, on bridges, and in
barns. Characterized by soft *coo-cuk-cuk-cuk-cooo* call.

Habitat

Introduced from Europe in the 1600s, the Rock Pigeon
is now found almost anywhere near human habitation.

Local Sites

The familiar beggar and street-cleaner is common in
almost every city and town, and large flocks live in
many farmyards.

FIELD NOTES The Rock Pigeon's variable colors, ranging
from rust red to all white to mosaic (inset), were
developed over centuries of near domestica-
tion. The pigeons that most resemble their
wild ancestors have a dark head and
neck, two black wing bars, a white
rump, and a black terminal band
on the tail.

Year-round | Adult

MOURNING DOVE

Zenaida macroura L 12" (31 cm)

FIELD MARKS

Gray-brown; black spots on upper wings; white tips on outer tail feathers show in flight

Trim-bodied; long pointed tail

Black spot on lower cheek; pinkish wash on neck.

Behavior
Generally a ground feeder, the Mourning Dove forages for grains, seeds, grasses, and insects. Like other *Columbidae*, it is able to slurp up water without tipping back its head. The Mourning Dove is aggressively territorial while nesting, but will gather into large roosting flocks after breeding season. Also known to produce multiple broods a season. Wings produce a fluttering whistle as the bird takes flight. Known for its mournful call, *oowooo-woo-woo-woo*, given by males during breeding season.

Habitat
Widespread and abundant, the Mourning Dove is found in a variety of habitats, but prefers open areas, often choosing suburban sites for feeding and nesting.

Local Sites
Abundant throughout the region, these birds can be found in virtually every habitat except deep forests.

FIELD NOTES The Mourning Dove, like other members of the family Columbidae, has the ability to produce "pigeon milk" in its crop lining. It regurgitates this substance to its young during their first few days. In appearance and nutritious content, it is remarkably similar to the milk of mammals.

Year-round | Adult

YELLOW-BILLED CUCKOO

Coccyzus americanus L 12" (31 cm)

FIELD MARKS

Gray-brown above, mostly white
below; yellow orbital ring

Decurved bill with dark upper
mandible and yellow lower

Underside of tail patterned in bold
black and white

Behavior

This shy species slips quietly through woodlands,
combing vegetation for caterpillars and insects. During
courtship, male climbs on female's shoulders to feed
her from above. Builds nest of grasses and moss on
horizontal tree limb. Unique song sounds hollow and
wooden, a rapid staccato *kuk-kuk-kuk,* usually descending to a *kakakowlp-kowlp* ending; it is often heard just
before a storm in spring and summer.

Habitat

Common in dense canopies of woods, orchards, and
streamside groves. Also inhabits tangles of swamp
edges. Winters in South America.

Local Sites

Look high in trees—or better yet, listen for these birds'
calls—in any woodland. Blackwater National Wildlife
Refuge or the C & O Canal Towpath are good locations.

FIELD NOTES The closely related Black-
billed Cuckoo, *Coccyzus erythropthalmus*
(inset), is known to sometimes lay its eggs
in the nests of Yellow-billeds. It is best distinguished by its dark bill and red eye ring.

Year-round | Adult rufous morph

EASTERN SCREECH-OWL

Megascops asio L 8.5" (22 cm)

FIELD MARKS

Small; with yellow eyes and pale tip on yellow-green bill

Rufous and gray morphs occur

Underparts marked by vertical streaks crossed by dark bars

Ear tufts prominent if raised

Behavior

Nocturnal; uses exceptional vision and hearing to hunt for mice, voles, shrews, and insects. Seeks out densest and thickest cover available for daytime roost and, if approached, will stretch its body, erect its ear tufts, and shut its eyes to blend into background. Nests in tree cavities about 10 to 30 feet up. Emits a series of quavering trills, descending in pitch, when defending territory; and a long, low-pitched trill around the nest site.

Habitat

Found in a wide variety of habitats including woodlots, forests, swamps, parks, and suburban gardens.

Local Sites

By far the most common owl in the region, it is even found in city parks such as Rock Creek Park in D.C. You will often hear a response, or lure a screech-owl into view, by imitating its call in any area with small woodlots surrounded by open space.

FIELD NOTES The region's smallest owl, only about the size of a robin, the Northern Saw-whet, *Aegolius acadicus* (inset: adult), is difficult to study due to its elusive nature and diminutive size. Recent surveys show that Saw-whets are more common in the state than previously thought, and banding programs indicate that fairly large numbers migrate throughout the region.

Year-round | Adult

GREAT HORNED OWL

Bubo virginianus L 22" (56 cm) WS 54" (137 cm)

FIELD MARKS

Mottled brownish gray above, densely barred below

Long ear tufts, or "horns"

Rust-colored facial disks

Yellow eyes; white chin and throat; buff-colored underwings

Behavior

Chiefly nocturnal. Watches from perch, then swoops down on prey, which includes cats, skunks, porcupines, birds, snakes, rodents, and frogs. Reuses abandoned nests of other large birds. Begins nesting by February, possibly to take advantage of winter-stressed prey. Territorial song, often sung in duet, consists of three to eight loud, deep hoots, the second and third often short and rapid. Song mostly heard at dusk and dawn.

Habitat

The most widespread owl in North America, the Great Horned Owl can be found in a wide variety of habitats including forests, cities, and farmlands.

Local Sites

Common throughout the region, listen for a Great Horned's call in any woodland. Blackwater National Wildlife Refuge and Deal Island Wildlife Management Area have good numbers that are easily seen.

FIELD NOTES Voracious predators, Great Horned Owls eat a variety of birds and medium-sized mammals. With no sense of smell, Great Horneds are one of the only predators that regularly attack skunks. Crows are also favored prey, and flocks of crows will aggressively try to drive owls away if they are found by day. This behavior is known as mobbing.

Year-round | Adult

BARRED OWL

Strix varia L 21" (53 cm)

FIELD MARKS

Large, chunky owl with dark eyes, darkly-ringed facial disk

Brown overall, with dark barring on upper breast and streaking below

Lacks ear tufts

Wings appear rounded in flight

Behavior

Pursues small mammals such as mice, squirrels, and rabbits by watching from perch, or by flying low over ground, sometimes hovering before dropping down to clutch prey in its talons. Nests in tree hollows. Call is a distinctive *who-cooks-for-you, who-cooks-for-you-all* or a drawn-out *hoo-ah*.

Habitat

Dense woodlands, mixed woods of rivers or swamps. Often sharing territory with the Great Horned, the Barred is much less aggressive and will steer clear of a Great Horned in its territory.

Local Sites

Common in mature woodlands regionwide, Barred Owls especially prefer swamps and wooded rivers, such as the Pocomoke or Patuxent.

FIELD NOTES Rarely seen except on farms, the Barn Owl, *Tyto alba* (inset), is true to its name and most often makes its nests in barns or silos, more rarely in old trees or rocky crevices. Its heart-shape face is unique; its call, a harsh screech. It is strictly nocturnal.

Year-round | Adult

COMMON NIGHTHAWK

Chordeiles minor L 9.5" (24 cm)

FIELD MARKS

Dark gray-brown mottled back; bold white bar across primaries

Long, pointed wings with pale spotting; tail slightly forked

Underparts whitish with bold dusky bars; bar on tail in males

Behavior
Hunts in flight, snaring insects; streamlined body allows agile aerial maneuvers. Drops lower jaw to create opening wide enough to take in even large moths. Skims over surface of lakes to drink. Roosts on the ground and on branches, posts, or roofs. Nests on the ground or on gravel rooftops. Male's wings make hollow booming sound during diving courtship display. Male gives a nasal *peent* in flight.

Habitat
Frequents woodlands, shrubby areas, and urban and suburban settings. Winters in South America.

Local Sites
Numbers have declined, but a few nest on rooftops in large cities, including Salisbury and Baltimore; nighthawks often hunt insects around the lights at Camden Yards. Look also for flocks migrating on August evenings along the Baltimore–D.C. corridor.

FIELD NOTES Another nighttime insect hunter of summer, the Whip-poor-will, *Caprimulgus vociferus* (inset: male), hunts in flight for moths and mosquitoes and roosts on the ground during the day. It is most easily identified in the field by its loud, melodious song: *WHIP poor WILL*.

Year-round | Adult

CHIMNEY SWIFT

Chaetura pelagica L 5.3" (13 cm)

FIELD MARKS
Short, cigar-shaped body

Long, pointed, narrow wings

Dark plumage, sooty gray overall

Short, stubby tail

Blackish gray bill, legs, feet

Behavior
Crisscrosses the sky with rapid wingbeats of long wings at impressive speeds, snatching up ants, termites, and spiders while in flight. Look for large groups of migrating Chimney Swifts circling above rooftops at dusk before dropping into chimneys or steeples to roost. Builds cup-shaped nest of small twigs glued together with dried saliva in chimneys, under eaves of barns, and in hollow trees. During aerial courtship, the male raises his wings into a sharp V. Call, given in flight, is a rapid, continual, high-pitched chattering.

Habitat
Often seen soaring over forested, open, suburban, and urban areas. Winters as far south as Peru.

Local Sites
These fast fliers are abundant summer residents throughout the region, even in downtown Baltimore and D.C.

FIELD NOTES The Chimney Swift once confined its nests to tree hollows and other natural sites. Over the centuries, it has adapted so well to artificial nesting sites such as chimneys, air shafts, vertical pipes, barns, and silos, that the species' numbers have increased dramatically, and natural nest sites are now very rare. It is the only swift seen regularly in the eastern U.S.

Year-round | Adult male

RUBY-THROATED HUMMINGBIRD

Archilochus colubris L 3.8" (9.7 cm)

FIELD MARKS
Metallic green above

Adult male has brilliant red gorget, black chin, whitish underparts, and dusky green sides

Female lacks gorget, has whitish throat and underparts, and a buffy wash on sides

Behavior
Probes flowers and hummingbird feeders for nectar by hovering, virtually still, in midair. Also feeds on small spiders and insects. When nectar is scarce, known to drink sap from wells made in tree trunks by sapsuckers. In spring, male Ruby-throateds arrive in breeding territory before females and engage in jousts to claim prime territory. In addition to the hum generated by its rapidly beating wings, it emits soft *tchiv* notes.

Habitat
Found in gardens and woodland edges throughout most of the eastern United States. Female builds nest on small, downsloping tree limbs.

Local Sites
Find the Ruby-throated drinking from summer flowers or hummingbird feeders throughout the region, sometimes, though rarely, into early October.

FIELD NOTES The Rufous Hummingbird, *Selasphorus rufus* (inset: male), is a western species that is appearing with increasing regularity. It and other rare hummingbirds appear from October to March when Ruby-throateds are not present.

Juvenile | Male

BELTED KINGFISHER

Ceryle alcyon L 13" (33 cm)

FIELD MARKS

Blue-gray head with large, shaggy crest

Blue-gray upperparts and breast band; white underparts and collar

Long, heavy, black bill

Female: chestnut sides and belly band

Behavior

Generally solitary and vocal, dives headfirst for fish from a waterside perch or after hovering above in order to line up on its target. Also feeds on insects, amphibians, and small reptiles. Monogamous pairs nest in burrows they dig together three or more feet into vertical earthen banks near watery habitats. Both male and female share in parenting duties as well. Mated pairs renew their relationship each breeding season with courtship rituals such as dramatic display flights, the male's feeding of the female, and vocalizations. Call is a loud, dry rattle; it is given when alarmed, to announce territory, or while in flight. Also makes harsh *caar* notes.

Habitat

Conspicuous along rivers, ponds, lakes, and coastal estuaries. Prefers partially wooded areas.

Local Sites

Look for Belted Kingfishers perched on branches overhanging the water at virtually every lake, creek, and river in the region. Patuxent Research Refuge and Blackwater National Wildlife Refuge are good bets.

FIELD NOTES The Belted Kingfisher female is one of the few birds in North America that is more colorful than her male counterpart, which lacks the female's chestnut band across the belly and chestnut sides and flanks.

Year-round | Adult male

RED-BELLIED WOODPECKER

Melanerpes carolina L 9.3" (24 cm)

FIELD MARKS

Black-and-white barred back

Red nape, extending onto crown
only on males

Mostly grayish underparts; small
reddish tinge on belly

Central tail feathers barred

Behavior

Climbs tree trunks by bracing itself with stiff tail,
taking strain off short legs. Uses chisel-shaped bill to
drill cavities in tree bark for nest holes and to extract
grubs and insects. Also feeds on worms, fruits, seeds,
and sap. Will visit backyard feeders for sunflower seeds
and peanut butter. Nests and roosts at night in tree
cavities. Call during breeding season is a rolling *churrr*.
Also gives a conversational *chiv chiv* all year.

Habitat

Common in open woodlands, forest edges, suburbs,
and parks.

Local Sites

These conspicuous residents are common in cities,
suburbs, parks, and woodlands throughout Maryland.
Rock Creek Park is the best place to see them in D.C.

FIELD NOTES The Red-headed Woodpecker,
Melanerpes erythrocephalus (inset: adult, left;
juvenile, right), shares much of the Red-
bellied's range, but is much less common.
The adult Red-headed is identified by its bright red
hood and its stark white rump and underparts. The
juvenile has a brownish hood and back.

Year-round | Adult male

YELLOW-BELLIED SAPSUCKER

Sphyrapicus varius **L 8.5" (22 cm)**

FIELD MARKS

Red forecrown on black and white head; chin, throat red on male, white on female

Back blackish with white barring; white rump and wing patch

Pale yellow wash on underparts

Behavior

Alone or in a pair, drills rows of evenly spaced holes in trees, then feeds on sap produced and insects attracted. Guards these wells fiercely from other birds and mammals. Also eats fruits, berries, and tree buds. Courtship ritual includes incessant loud drumming by both male and female, *hoy-hoy* cries, and dual tapping at nest entrance. Though often silent, the Yellow-bellied sometimes makes a low, plaintive *meeww* call, or a territorial call of *quee-ark*.

Habitat

The most highly migratory of all North American woodpeckers, found in deciduous and mixed forests.

Local Sites

The Yellow-bellied Sapsucker is found regionwide in migration and winter. Look in any forest, such as those along the C & O Canal Towpath, the Pocomoke River, or at Rock Creek Park in D.C.

FIELD NOTES The bone and muscle structure of a woodpecker's head is an effective shock absorber; a necessary adaptation for a bird that spends its time drilling into hard wood. Similarly, a stiff tail and sharp claws help to maintain the bird's upright position against a tree trunk. Notice how a woodpecker's tail braces the bird; a much needed support to maintain its vertical perches.

Year-round | Adult female

DOWNY WOODPECKER

Picoides pubescens L 6.8" (17 cm)

FIELD MARKS

Black cap, ear patch, moustachial stripe; black wings spotted white

Blaze of white on back

White tuft in front of eyes; whitish underparts

Red occipital patch on male

Behavior
The smallest woodpecker in North America, forages mainly on insects, larvae, and eggs. Readily visits back-yard feeders for sunflower seeds and suet. Will also consume poison-ivy berries. Small size enables the Downy to forage on very small, thin limbs. Nests in cavities of dead trees. Both male and female stake territorial claims with their drumming. Call is a high-pitched but soft *pik*. Also gives a high, accelerating whinny, *kee-kee-kee-kee.*

Habitat
Found in suburbs, parks, and orchards, as well as forests and woodlands.

Local Sites
The Downy is easy to find in any woodland, even in cities. Suet feeders attract them readily in winter.

FIELD NOTES The larger and less common Hairy Woodpecker, *Picoides villosus* (inset: male), is similarly marked but has a bill as long as its head and a sharper, louder, lower-pitched call. It also tends to stay on tree trunks or larger limbs than the Downy. Note as well the all-white outer tail feathers of the Hairy Woodpecker; the Downy's outer tail feathers are often spotted black.

Year-round | Adult female "Yellow-shafted"

NORTHERN FLICKER

Colaptes auratus **L** 12.5" (32 cm)

FIELD MARKS

White rump, yellowish underwing

Brown, barred back, cream underparts with black spotting, and black crescent bib

Gray crown, tan face, red crescent on nape, and, on male, black moustachial stripe

Behavior
An insectivore, the flicker forages mostly on the ground, primarily for ants. It is at least partially migratory, traveling in the winter in pursuit of food. Nests in cavities, and will drill into almost any wooden surface, including utility poles and houses. Bows to its partner before engaging in courtship of exaggerated wing and tail movements. Call a single, loud *klee-yer* heard year-round, or a long series of *wick wick wick wick*—sometimes lasting 15 seconds—in breeding season.

Habitat
Found in open woodlands and wooded suburban areas.

Local Sites
These large, loud woodpeckers are found in any woodland. Unlike most other woodpecker species, they can often be seen poking into the grass for grubs and ants on lawns. Check out migration sites such as Assateague Island where 100 or more can be seen daily in October.

FIELD NOTES The western, or "Red-shafted," form of Northern Flicker has pinkish underwings, a grayish face, and a red moustachial stripe on the male. Only "Yellow-shafted" Flickers occur in Maryland and D.C., but hybrids, which may show some intermediate characteristics of both forms, have been recorded.

Year-round | Adult male

PILEATED WOODPECKER

Dryocopus pileatus L 16.5" (42 cm)

FIELD MARKS

Almost entirely black on back and wings when perched

Black, white, and red striped head; red "moustache" on male

Red cap extends to bill on male

Juvenile browner overall

Behavior

Drills long, distinctively rectangular holes on tree trunks, searching for beetle larvae and other insects. Also digs into ground, stumps, and fallen logs, feeding on carpenter ants, beetles, acorns, seeds, and fruit. Nests in cavities excavated in dead or live trees, sometimes utility poles. Calls include a loud *wuk* note and a long, irregularly delivered series of *kee kee kee kee*. Also known for slow, but powerfully loud, territorial drumming, which can be heard a mile or more away.

Habitat

Prefers dense, mature forests; also found in smaller woodlots and some parks.

Local Sites

The region's largest and loudest woodpecker is traditionally a denizen of deep forests, but it is increasingly found visiting and nesting in small woodland tracts. The Pocomoke River drainage, C & O Canal Towpath, and much of Garrett County all have large populations.

FIELD NOTES The excavations of the Pileated are so extensive and deep that they may fell small trees. These holes can also attract other species, such as wrens and other woodpeckers, which use the large holes both for foraging and nesting.

Year-round | Adult

EASTERN PHOEBE

Sayornis phoebe L 7" (18 cm)

FIELD MARKS
Brownish gray above, darkest on head, wings, and tail; dark bill; lacks distinct wing bars

Underparts mostly white with pale olive wash on sides and breast

Fresh fall birds washed with yellow on belly

Behavior
Flicks tail constantly when perched, looking for flying insects to chase and snare in midair. Also easts small fish, berries, and fruit. Often builds delicate cup-like nest under bridges, in eaves, or in the rafters of old buildings, almost always near running water. Distinctive song is a rough, whistled *schree-dip,* followed by a descending *schree-brrr,* often repeated when male is attempting to lure a mate. Call is a sharp *tsip.*

Habitat
Found in woodlands, farmlands, and suburbs.

Local Sites
Look for them fly-catching near old buildings, bridges, and other man-made structures anywhere in the region, usually arriving in March and departing in October. A few winter in the region, particularly on the Eastern Shore.

FIELD NOTES Though very similarly plumaged, the Eastern Phoebe is distinguished from the Eastern Wood-Pewee, *Contopus virens* (inset), by its habit of constantly pumping its tail when perched. The wood-pewee tends to perch motionless. In addition, the wood-pewee's lower mandible is a dull orange, and it has two thin whitish wing bars.

Year-round | Adult

GREAT CRESTED FLYCATCHER

Myiarchus crinitus L 8" (20 cm)

FIELD MARKS

Gray face and breast contrasts with bright yellow belly and undertail coverts

Olive green above and on crest

Mostly rufous inner webs of tail feathers

Behavior

Forages high in tall trees, picking insects from foliage or snaging them in midair. During courtship, the male chases the female near a chosen nesting cavity, which is usually another bird's abandoned cavity or a birdbox. Male rarely leaves a fertile female's side and defends territory from other males in heated midair battles. Leans forward and bobs head if agitated. Calls include a loud, hoarse, ascending *whee-eep*, a softer *purr-it*, and a series of *whit* notes. Sings a continuous series of *whee-eep*s around dawn.

Habitat

Found in open deciduous and mixed woodlands, including parks and suburbs. Winters for the most part in Central and South America.

Local Sites

Common regionwide in breeding season, these large flycatchers prefer open and semi-open forests. Blackwater National Wildlife Refuge, the Pocomoke River, and the C & O Canal Towpath are all areas where it is common.

FIELD NOTES The Great Crested Flycatcher has traditionally decorated its nest with shed pieces of snakeskin, but these days it will make do with cellophane, plastic wrap, and onion skins.

Year-round | Adult

EASTERN KINGBIRD

Tyrannus tyrannus L 8.5" (22 cm)

FIELD MARKS

Black head, slate gray back

White terminal band on black tail

Underparts white except for pale gray wash across breast

Orange-red crown patch visible only when displaying

Behavior
Waits on perch until it spots prey, then darts out to snare it in midair. Feeds primarily on flying insects. May also hover to pick food from foliage. Males court with erratic hovering, swooping, and circling, revealing hidden crown patch. Builds cup-shaped nest near the end of a tree branch, sometimes on a post or stump. Emits raspy *zeer* call when feeding or defending. Sings a complex, repeated series of notes and trills at dawn.

Habitat
Found in woodland clearings, farms, orchards, and field edges, usually near lakes, ponds and waterways. Winters in South America.

Local Sites
One of the more common roadside birds in the region in summer, look for kingbirds on telephone wires especially, open areas such as Lilypons Water Gardens are ideal. They are present only from May to August.

FIELD NOTES Living up to its Latin name, which means "tyrant of tyrants," the Eastern Kingbird will actively defend its nest, sometimes pecking at and even pulling feathers from the backs of hawks, crows, and vultures.

Year-round | Adult

RED-EYED VIREO

Vireo olivaceus L 6" (15 cm)

FIELD MARKS
Blue-gray crown

White eyebrow, bordered above and below in black

Olive back, darker wings and tail

White underparts

Ruby red eye, visible at close range

Behavior
Searches through foliage for fruits, berries, and insects, especially caterpillars. Sometimes hovers to snatch food from high branches. Male known to chase female during courtship, sometimes even pinning her to the ground. Builds nest of grass and forest debris on horizontal tree limb. Song is a variable series of deliberate, short phrases, *cheer-o-wit, cher-ee, chit-a-wit, de-o,* sung nearly nonstop from dawn through dusk and while brooding, foraging, roosting, and even while swallowing. Call is a whining, down-slurred *myahh.*

Habitat
Found in the forest canopies of deciduous woodlands.

Local Sites
Perhaps the most common forest bird in the region, but not commonly seen as it stays high in the trees. Listen for it in any forest area from May to September.

FIELD NOTES In addition to its eye color, the White-eyed Vireo, *Vireo griseus* (inset: adult), differs from the Red-eyed Vireo in its bold white wing-bars and yellow spectacles. During summer, the White-eyed inhabits thickets and tangles regionwide and is best found by its loud song: *Quick, pick up the beer check! Quick!*

Year-round | Adult

BLUE JAY

Cyanocitta cristata L 11" (28 cm)

FIELD MARKS
Blue crest and back

Black barring and white patches
on blue wings and tail

Black collar line on grayish white
underparts extends onto nape

Black bill, legs, and feet

Behavior
Often seen singly or in small family groups, foraging
for insects, acorns and other nuts, berries, and seeds.
Will also raid nests for eggs and nestlings of other
species. A bobbing display may be observed during
courtship. Builds nest in oak and beech trees 5 to 20
feet up. The noisy, bold Blue Jay gives a diverse array of
vocalizations, including a loud, piercing alarm call of
jay jay jay, a musical *yo-ghurt,* and imitations of several
hawk species, particularly the Red-shouldered Hawk.

Habitat
Found in fragmented woodlands, parks, and suburban
backyards. Some birds are migratory, while others are
year-round residents.

Local Sites
Loud, flashy, and ubiquitous, the Blue Jay is common
throughout the region. In fall they migrate down the
ridges of western Maryland, sometimes in large flocks.

FIELD NOTES A resourceful feeder, the Blue Jay will store acorns
in the ground for winter months when food is scarce. As many of
these acorns are never recovered, this practice is a major factor
in the establishment and distribution of oak forests throughout
the jay's range.

Year-round | Adult

AMERICAN CROW

Corvus brachyrhynchos L 17.5" (45 cm)

FIELD MARKS
Black, iridescent plumage overall
Broad wings and squared off tail
Long, heavy, black bill
Brown eyes
Black legs and feet

Behavior
Often forages, roosts, and travels in flocks. Individuals take turns at sentry duty while others feed on insects, garbage, grain, mice, eggs, and young birds. Known to noisily mob large raptors, such as eagles, hawks, and Great Horned Owls, in order to drive them from its territory. Because its bill is ineffective on tough hides, crows wait for another predator—or an automobile—to open a carcass before dining. Studies have shown the crow's ability to count, solve puzzles, and retain information. Nests in shrubs, trees, or on poles. Readily identified by its familiar *caw* call.

Habitat
Widely distributed; lives in a variety of habitats.

Local Sites
Few species are as varied in habitat as this large "song-bird," which is well-known to birders and nonbirders alike and common in forests, fields, towns, and cities.

FIELD NOTES The closely related and similarly plumaged Fish Crow, *Corvus ossifragus,* is smaller than the American Crow, but is best told apart by its high, nasal, two-syllable *ca-hah* call. Common in Chesapeake Bay marshes; also ranges west to Frederick County and along the Potomac River to Frostburg.

Year-round | Adult

COMMON RAVEN

Corvus corax L 24" (61 cm)

FIELD MARKS

Glossy black overall with iridescent violet sheen

Long, heavy, black bill with long nasal bristles on upper mandible

Thick, shaggy throat feathers

Wedge-shaped tail

Behavior
Forages on a variety of food, from worms and insects to rodents and eggs to carrion and refuse. Small groups are known to hunt together in order to overcome prey that is too large for just one bird to take. Monogamous for life, these birds engage in acrobatic courtship flights of synchronized dives, chases, and tumbles. Builds nest high up in trees or on cliffs. Calls are variable, but include a low, drawn out *kraaah* and a nasal *brooonk*.

Habitat
Found in a variety of habitats, but most abundant in forested areas at high elevations.

Local Sites
Ravens are entirely restricted to mountainous areas of western Maryland. Check for them at Swallow Falls State Park, Rocky Gap, or virtually anywhere from Frederick County west.

FIELD NOTES The raven is considerably larger than the crow, but this can be difficult to discern from a distance. Look for the raven's wedge-shaped tail, as opposed to the squared-off tail of the crow. The raven is also much more likely to soar on flattened wings than the crow, which flies with steady wing beats.

Year-round | Adult male

HORNED LARK

Eremophila alpestris L 6.8-7.8" (17-20 cm)

FIELD MARKS

White or yellowish forehead bordered by black band, which ends in hornlike tufts on adult males

Black cheek stripes, bill, and bib

Yellow or white throat and underparts; brown or rufous upperparts

Behavior

The only lark native to North America forages on the ground mainly on seeds, grain, and some insects. The Horned Lark walks or runs, rather than hops, and it seldom alights on trees or bushes. Outside breeding season, the larks organize into flocks. Uses its bill and feet with long hind claws to create shallow depressions for nesting. Song begins with two or three *chit* notes, then flows into a rapid, jumbled twittering that rises slightly in pitch. Calls include a high-pitched *tsee-titi*.

Habitat

Found in open agricultural fields, grasslands, dirt fields, sod farms, airports, gravel ridges, and shores.

Local Sites

Extensive farmlands of the Eastern Shore are the best areas for Horned Larks in the region. Dirt fields between Cambridge and Blackwater National Wildlife Refuge are consistently productive year-round.

FIELD NOTES The male Horned Lark performs a spectacular flight display, ascending several hundred feet, circling and singing for a bit, then plummeting headfirst toward the ground, flaring his wings open for landing at the last second. With horns upraised, he then struts for the female, having proven his aerial agility.

Year-round | Adult male

PURPLE MARTIN

Progne subis L 8" (20 cm)

FIELD MARKS

Male is dark, glossy purplish blue

Female has bluish gray upper-parts; grayish breast and belly

Long, pointed wings; forked tail

Dark eyes, bill, legs, and feet

Juvenile brown above, gray below

Behavior
Forages almost exclusively in flight, darting for wasps, bees, dragonflies, winged ants, and other large insects. Long, sharply pointed wings and substantial tail allow it graceful maneuverability in the air. Capable of drinking, even bathing, in flight by skimming just over water's surface and dipping bill, or breast, into water. Nests almost exclusively in man-made multi-dwelling martin houses. Song is a series of croaks and gurgles.

Habitat
Found in open areas near martin houses and water. Winters in South America.

Local Sites
Colonies of Purple Martins can be found at nest boxes anywhere in the region except the far west. Migrant flocks stop by in August, with a particularly large concentration at Vienna, along the Nanticoke River.

FIELD NOTES Purple Martins in eastern North America are highly dependent on man-made nesting houses, which can hold many pairs of breeding adults. The tradition of making martin houses from hollowed gourds originated with Native Americans, who found that this sociable bird helped reduce insects around villages and crops. The practice was adopted by colonists, and martins have accordingly prospered for many generations.

Year-round | Adult

TREE SWALLOW

Tachycineta bicolor L 5.8" (15 cm)

FIELD MARKS
Dark, glossy, greenish blue above

White below

Slightly notched tail

Long, pointed, blackish wings

Juvenile gray-brown above with
dusky wash on its breast

Behavior
During migration, seen in huge flocks or perched in
long rows on branches and wires. Darts over fields or
water to catch insects in flight, but switches to diet of
berries and plant buds during colder months, when
insects are less abundant. Nests in tree cavities, fence
posts, barn eaves, and man-made birdhouses. Song is a
rapid, extended series of variable chirping notes—*chrit,
pleet, euree, cheet, chrit, pleet.*

Habitat
Found in wooded habitats near water, or where dead
trees provide nest holes in fields, marshes, or towns.

Local Sites
Migrants are found regionwide, but nesting birds are
spotty in distribution. Blackwater National Wildlife
Refuge, Lilypons Water Gardens, and New Germany
State Park are good in summer. Flocks at Assateague
Island may number in the thousands in October.

FIELD NOTES Among the world's swallows, the Tree Swallow
more regularly feeds on plant material and has a particular
fondness for waxy bayberries, for which it has developed a
special digesting ability. These adaptations allow it to migrate
north earlier than other swallows and linger later in the fall.

Year-round | Adult

BARN SWALLOW

Hirundo rustica L 6.8" (17 cm)

FIELD MARKS

Long, deeply forked, dark tail

Iridescent deep blue upperparts;
cinnamon to whitish underparts,
paler on female

Rusty brown forehead and throat;
dark blue-black breast band

Behavior

An exuberant flyer, often seen in small flocks skimming
low over the surface of a field or pond, taking insects in
midair. Will follow tractors and lawn mowers to feed
on flushed insects. An indicator of coming storms, as
barometric pressure changes cause the bird to fly lower
to the ground. Has adapted to humans to the extent
that it now nests almost exclusively in structures such
as barns, bridges, culverts, and garages. Call in flight is
a high-pitched, squeaky *chee-jit*. Song is a long series of
squeaky warbles interrupted by nasal, grating rattles.

Habitat

Frequents open farms and fields, especially those near
water. Widely distributed all over the world.

Local Sites

Virtually every farm in Maryland hosts a colony of
these abundant swallows in barns and storage buildings
during the summer breeding season.

FIELD NOTES The Cliff Swallow, *Petrochelidon
pyrrhonota* (inset), can also be found in summer
nesting under bridges and eaves or foraging over
fields and ponds. In flight, it is best distinguished
from the Barn Swallow by its squarish tail and buffy
rump. Its pale forehead is a distinctive field mark as well.

Year-round | Adult

CAROLINA CHICKADEE

Poecile carolinensis L 4.8" (12 cm)

FIELD MARKS

Black cap and bib

White cheeks, gray upperparts

Whitish underparts, with buff-gray wash on flanks and lower belly

Short black bill, blackish legs

Short, slightly notched tail

Behavior

Seldom descends to ground, energetically forages among leaves and twigs for moths, caterpillars, and insects. Often hangs upside down to glean underside of foliage. Visits backyard feeders for seeds and suet. After breeding season it joins in mixed foraging flocks with nuthatches, titmice, Downy Woodpeckers, and other small birds. Best distinguished from Black-capped Chickadee by call, a higher, faster version of *chick-a-dee-dee-dee*. Song is a four-note whistle, *fee-bee fee-bay*.

Habitat

Woodland edges and clearings, oak forests, wooded city parks, and suburban yards. Nests in old woodpecker holes, man-made nesting boxes, and natural crevices.

Local Sites

Chickadees are conspicuous in woods and at feeders regionwide. Any chickadee from Frederick County east is sure to be a Carolina.

FIELD NOTES The Black-capped Chickadee, *Poecile atricapilla* (inset), has plumage nearly identical to the Carolina's, but its wing coverts are edged in white; also, its call is slower. It replaces the Carolina Chickadee in Allegany and Garrett Counties; they hybridize where their ranges narrowly overlap in Washington County.

Year-round | Adult

TUFTED TITMOUSE

Baeolophus bicolor L 6.3" (16 cm)

FIELD MARKS

Gray above, whitish below

Russet wash on sides

Gray crest; blackish forehead

Pale spots around dark eyes

Juvenile has gray forehead and paler crest

Behavior
Very active forager in trees, seeking insects, spiders, snails, berries, and seeds. Known to hold a nut with its feet and pound it open with its bill. A common visitor to backyard feeders, especially fond of sunflower seeds and suet. Male feeds female in courtship. Nests in natural cavities, woodpecker holes, man-made boxes, and sometimes in fence posts. Song is a loud, whistled *peto-peto-peto* or *wheedle-wheedle-wheedle*. Employs up to ten different calls, including a harsh *zhee zhee zhee,* which it uses to keep foraging groups together.

Habitat
Found in open forests, woodlands, groves, and orchards, as well as urban and suburban parks.

Local Sites
These lively chatterers are easy to find year-round in forests, woodlands, and suburban parks everywhere in the region.

FIELD NOTES Unintimidated by proximity to humans, the Tufted Titmouse will approach people who make a squeaking sound or *pish,* a useful tool for a birder. It is even known to swoop down and pluck hair directly from a human's scalp for use in its nest.

Year-round | Adult male

WHITE-BREASTED NUTHATCH

Sitta carolinensis L 5.8" (15 cm)

FIELD MARKS

White face and breast; black cap

Blue-gray upperparts; wing and tail feathers tipped in white

Rust or brown colored underparts near legs

White pattern on blue-black tail

Behavior

Creeps down tree trunks or large branches in search of insects and spiders. Will also gather nuts and seeds, jam them into bark, and hammer or "hatch" the food open with bill. Roosts in tree cavities, and sometimes even in crevices of bark in summer. Builds nest in abandoned woodpecker holes or in natural cavities inside decaying trees. Song is a rapid series of nasal whistles on one pitch: *whi-whi-whi-whi-whi-whi*. Call is a slow, low-pitched, nasal *yank, yank*.

Habitat

Found in deciduous or mixed woods.

Local Sites

These upside-down tree climbers are present year-round in large forests, small woodlands, urban parks, and backyards throughout the region.

FIELD NOTES In winter, the White-breasted often joins mixed-species foraging groups with the Red-breasted Nuthatch, *Sitta canadensis* (inset: female, top; male, bottom). Though similar in behavior, the less common Red-breasted is noticeably smaller and has rust-colored underparts, darker on the males. The Red-breasted forages on small branches and outer twigs and prefers conifers.

Year-round | Adult

BROWN-HEADED NUTHATCH

Sitta pusilla L 4.5" (11 cm)

FIELD MARKS
Brown cap; pale nape spot
Blue-gray above, dull buff below
White cheeks, chin, and throat
Dark, narrow eyeline borders cap
Straight black bill

Behavior
A small and usually noisy nuthatch that feeds in pairs or small flocks. One of the few bird species known to use tools, forages in pine tree bark for insects, using one piece of bark to dislodge another. Also consumes large numbers of seeds from pinecones when insects are scarce. Forms flocks with chickadees, warblers, and other small landbirds. Call is a repeated double note like the squeak of a rubber duck. Feeding flocks also give twittering, chirping *bit bit bit* calls.

Habitat
Fairly widespread and locally common in pine wood-lands and pine plantations. Nests in hollow trees, stumps, or man-made bird boxes.

Local Sites
This southeastern specialty can be found in pine woods of the lower Eastern Shore. Blackwater National Wildlife Refuge and Deal Island Wildlife Management Area support the species in good numbers.

FIELD NOTES Maryland lies at the extreme northern limit of the species' range, but it has historically been quite common in loblolly pine forests of the lower Eastern Shore. Recent count data, however, show a significant decline throughout Maryland. Although the decline is not easily explained, the overall health of the pine woods may be to blame.

Year-round | Adult

BROWN CREEPER

Certhia americana L 5.3" (13 cm)

FIELD MARKS

Mottled, streaky brown above

White eyebrow stripe

White underparts

Long, thin decurved bill

Long, graduated tail

Behavior

Camouflaged by streaked brown plumage, it climbs upward from the base of a tree, then flies to a lower place on another tree in search of insects and larvae in tree bark. Long, decurved bill helps it to dig prey out of tree bark; its stiff tail feathers serving as a prop against the trunk. Forages by itself in general, unless part of a mixed-species flock in winter. Builds nests behind loose bark of dead or dying trees. Call is a soft, sibilant, almost inaudible *seee*. Song is a high-pitched *seee seeed-see sideeu,* or a similar variation.

Habitat

Found mostly in heavily forested areas. May wander into suburban and urban parks in winter.

Local Sites

These tiny, tree-trunk climbers are well camouflaged against the bark, so look for them carefully. Swallow Falls State Park, the Pocomoke River, and the C & O Canal are consistent wintering locations where the species may even be found breeding on rare occasion.

FIELD NOTES If the creeper suspects the presence of a predator, it will spread its wings and tail, press its body tight against the trunk of a tree, and remain completely motionless. In this pose, its camouflaged plumage makes it almost invisible.

Year-round | Adult

CAROLINA WREN

Thryothorus ludovicianus L 5.5" (14 cm)

FIELD MARKS
Deep rusty brown above with
dark brown bars

Prominent white eye stripe

Warm buff below

White chin and throat

Long, slightly decurved bill

Behavior

Pokes around on ground with its decurved bill, looking
for insects, spiders, snails, fruits, berries, and seeds. A
pair stays together in its territory throughout the year.
Nests in any open cavity of suitable size, including
woodpecker holes, barn rafters, mailboxes, flowerpots,
even boots left outside. From its perch at any time of
day or season, male sings rich, melodious song of
repeated phrases, sometimes starting or ending with a
single note—*chip mediator mediator mediator meep*—
to which female may respond with a low rattle.

Habitat

Found in underbrush of moist woodlands and swamps,
and around human habitation on farms, in wooded
suburbs, and less frequently in city parks.

Local Sites

Well adapted to human activities, the noisy Carolina
Wren is ubiquitous regionwide, although it is rare in
Garrett County of far western Maryland.

FIELD NOTES The northern limit of the Carolina Wren's range will
expand and contract in response to the severity of winter
weather. In mild years, it sometimes extends its range into
Canada, but is pushed back by the next harsh winter.

Year-round | Adult

HOUSE WREN

Troglodytes aedon L 4.8" (12 cm)

FIELD MARKS
Grayish or brown upperparts

Fine black barring on wings
and tail

Pale gray underparts

Pale faint eye ring, eyebrow

Thin, slightly decurved bill

Behavior
Noisy, conspicuous, and relatively tame, with its tail
often cocked upward. Gleans insects and spiders from
vegetation. Forages at a variety of levels, including high
up in trees. Male begins construction on a number of
possible nests in any crevice of suitable size. Female
joins him, inspects the nests, and chooses one to complete. Sings exuberantly in a cascade of bubbling,
down-slurred trills. Call is a rough *chek-chek,* often
running into a chatter.

Habitat
Found in open woodlands and thickets, and in shrub-
bery around farms, parks, and suburban gardens.

Local Sites
Thickets, woodland edges, shrubby fields, and backyard
nesting boxes host summer-breeding pairs throughout
the region, especially in rural areas and small towns.

FIELD NOTES The Winter Wren, *Troglodytes troglodytes* (inset), has a
short, stubby tail and darker barring on its belly than the House
Wren. Its song is a rapid series of melodious
trills, and its sharp *chimp-chimp* call is distinctive. The secretive Winter Wren winters in
dense brush, especially along stream banks
in moist woods.

Year-round | Adult male

GOLDEN-CROWNED KINGLET

Regulus satrapa L 4" (10 cm)

FIELD MARKS

Yellow crown patch bordered in black; tuft of orange feathers within yellow on male

Olive green upperparts, pale buff underparts

Broad whitish eyebrow; two whitish wing bars

Behavior

Gleans insects and larvae from bark and leaves, reaching into tiny recesses with its short, straight bill. Also drinks tree sap, sometimes following sapsuckers to fresh drill holes. Constructs a spherical nest of lichen, moss, bark, and feathers. Song is almost inaudibly high, consisting of a series of *tsii* notes becoming louder and chattering toward the end. Call is high, thin *tsii tsii tsii*.

Habitat

Found in dense, coniferous and mixed woodlands.

Local Sites

Most conspicuous on Assateague Island in October, wintering birds can be found in pines regionwide. Breeders are restricted to western Maryland conifers, as at New Germany State Park.

FIELD NOTES The closely related Ruby-crowned Kinglet, *Regulus calendula* (inset: male, left; female, right), may be seen in the same mixed-species foraging flock in winter as the Golden-crowned. It is distinguished by its plainer face and its husky *ji-dit* call. The red crown patch of the male Ruby-crowned is exposed only when it is agitated.

Year-round | Adult male

EASTERN BLUEBIRD

Sialia sialis L 7" (18 cm)

FIELD MARKS
Male is bright blue above

Female is a grayer blue above,
duller below

Chestnut throat, breast, flanks,
and sides of neck

White belly and undertail coverts

Behavior
Hunts from elevated perch in the open, dropping to the
ground to seize crickets, grasshoppers, and spiders. Has
been observed pouncing on prey it has spotted from as
many as 130 feet away. In winter, forms small flocks
and roosts communally at night in tree cavities or nest
boxes. During courtship, male shows vivid coloring on
his side during wing-waving displays beside a chosen
nesting site. Nests in woodpecker holes, hollow trees or
stumps, and in nest boxes. Call is a musical, rising *too-
lee,* extended in song to *too too-lee too-lee.*

Habitat
Found in open woodlands, meadows with scattered
trees, farmlands, and orchards.

Local Sites
Their numbers are increasing steadily regionwide.
Blackwater National Wildlife Refuge and Lilypons
Water Gardens have a number of active nest boxes.

FIELD NOTES The Eastern Bluebird's serious decline in decades
past is due largely to competition for nesting sites with two introduced species, the European Starling and the House Sparrow.
Specially designed bluebird nest boxes provided by concerned
birders have contributed to a promising comeback.

Year-round | Adult

HERMIT THRUSH

Catharus guttatus L 6.8" (17cm)

FIELD MARKS

Gray-brown upperparts; white to buffy underparts with dense spotting mostly on breast

Reddish tail contrasts with upperparts

Whitish eye ring; dark lateral throat streak

Behavior

The Hermit Thrush is a shy, terrestrial bird that forages on the forest floor for insects or ascends into bushes in search of berries. When interrupted it flies up into a low bush, flicking its wings nervously and slowly raising and lowering its tail. Common call is a blackbird-like *chuck,* often doubled; song is a serene series of clear, flutelike notes, the phrases repeated at different pitches, lending it a lyrical quality.

Habitat

For breeding, coniferous forests typically in areas of relatively little undergrowth. In winter and migration uses a wide variety of habitats, but always with forest or brushy cover nearby, especially in shady river valleys.

Local Sites

Most common in winter in wet bottomland woods, especially in stands of American holly. Nesters may be found in western Maryland, such as at Swallow Falls State Park.

FIELD NOTES The most common summering thrush, Wood Thrush, *Hylocichla mustelina* (inset), is found in mature deciduous woods regionwide from May to September. Rarely overlaps with Hermit Thrush, but when it does, its thick black spotting and bold white eye ring are distinctive.

Year-round | Adults

AMERICAN ROBIN

Turdus migratorius L 10" (25 cm)

FIELD MARKS
Brick red underparts, paler in
female, spotted in juvenile

Brownish gray above with darker
head and tail

White throat and lower belly

Broken white eye ring; yellow bill

Behavior
Best known and largest of the thrushes, often seen on
suburban lawns, hopping about and cocking its head
in search of earthworms. Gleans butterflies, damselflies,
and other flying insects from foliage and sometimes
takes prey in flight. Robins also eat fruit, especially in
fall and winter. This broad plant and animal diet makes
them one of the most successful and wide-ranging
thrushes. Nests in shrubs, trees, and even on sheltered
windowsills. Calls include a low, mellow *pup*, a doubled
or tripled *chok* or *tut*, and a sharp *kli ki ki ki ki*. Song is
a clear, variable *cheerily cheery cheerily cheery*.

Habitat
Common and widespread, forages on lawns and in
woodlands. Winters mostly near thickets, woodland
edges, and urban parks rich in fruit-bearing trees.

Local Sites
Look for the American Robin in your own backyard.
The species is everywhere, including the most crowded
big cities.

FIELD NOTES The juvenile robin, which can be seen every year
between May and September, has a paler breast, like the female
of the species, but its underparts are heavily spotted with brown.
Look as well for the buff fringes on its back and wing feathers
and its short, pale buff eyebrow.

Year-round | Adult

NORTHERN MOCKINGBIRD

Mimus polyglottos L 10" (25 cm)

FIELD MARKS
Gray overall; darker above

White wing patches and outer tail feathers, which flash conspicuously in flight

Long, blackish wings and tail

Short, black bill

Behavior
The pugnacious Northern Mockingbird will protect its territory against other birds as well as dogs, cats, and humans. Has a varied diet that includes berries, grasshoppers, spiders, snails, and earthworms. An expert mimic, the mockingbird is known for variety of song, learning and imitating calls of many other species and animals. Typically repeats a song's phrases three times before beginning a new one. Call is a loud, sharp *check*.

Habitat
Resides in a variety of habitats, including cities, towns and suburbs. Feeds and nests close to the ground, in thickets, trees, or shrubby vegetation.

Local Sites
One of region's most widespread and common birds, largely absent from westernmost Maryland.

FIELD NOTES One of the only mimics to truly rival the mockingbird in breadth and variety of imitations is the Gray Catbird, *Dumetella carolinensis* (inset). In addition to its catlike *mew,* the catbird can reproduce calls of other birds, of amphibians, even of machinery, and incorporate them into its song. It is a common breeder regionwide.

Year-round | Adult

BROWN THRASHER

Toxostoma rufum L 11.5" (29 cm)

FIELD MARKS

Reddish brown above

Pale buff to white below with heavy dark streaking

Long, reddish brown tail

Yellow eyes; dark, decurved bill

Two white wing bars

Behavior

Forages through leaf litter for insects, fruit, and grain; finds additional prey by digging with decurved bill. Courtship involves little fanfare, the whole process consisting of one or both birds picking up leaves or twigs and dropping them in front of the other. Nests in bushes, on ground, or in low trees. Sings from an exposed perch a long series of varied melodious phrases, each one given two or three times. Calls include a loud, smacking *spuck* and a low *churr*.

Habitat

Found in hedgerows, dense brush, and woodland edges.

Local Sites

Look for these large, loud songsters during breeding season in brushy fields and woodland edges throughout the region. Winter birds are much harder to find, but occur in small numbers in the East.

FIELD NOTES A very creative vocalizer, the Brown Thrasher has the ability to mimic other birds, but more often sings its own song—it's got enough of them. It has been reported that the Brown Thrasher has the largest song repertoire of any North American bird; more than 1,100 types have been recorded. The number of songs a male can sing may be an indicator of status to females seeking a mate.

Nonbreeding | Adult

EUROPEAN STARLING

Sturnus vulgaris L 8.5" (22 cm)

FIELD MARKS

Iridescent black breeding plumage

Buffy tips on back, tail feathers

Fall feathers tipped in white,
giving speckled appearance

Yellow bill in summer; its base is
pale blue on male, pink on female

Behavior

A social and aggressive bird, feeds on a variety of food,
ranging from invertebrates—such as snails, worms, and
spiders—to fruit, berries, grains, seeds, and garbage.
Probes ground, opening bill to create small holes and
expose prey. Usually seen in flocks, except while nesting
in cavities, ranging from crevices in urban settings to
woodpecker holes and nest boxes. Imitates calls of
other species and emits high-pitched notes, including
squeaks, hisses, whistles, rattles, and wheezes.

Habitat

The adaptable starling thrives in a variety of habitats
near humans, including urban centers and farmland.

Local Sites

Big cities, towns, and farmlands are all home to this
ubiquitous import from Europe. Look for immense
flocks that gather during early fall and winter in rural
areas of the region.

FIELD NOTES A Eurasian species introduced into New York's
Central Park in 1890, the European Starling has since spread
throughout the U.S. and Canada. Abundant, bold, and aggressive, starlings often compete for and take over nest sites of other
native birds, including bluebirds, Wood Ducks, a variety of
woodpeckers, Tree Swallows, and Purple Martins.

Year-round | Adult

CEDAR WAXWING

Bombycilla cedrorum L 7.3" (19 cm)

FIELD MARKS

Distinctive sleek crest

Black mask bordered in white

Brownish head, back, breast, and sides; pale yellow belly; gray rump

Yellow terminal tail band

May have red, waxy tips on wings

Behavior

Eats the most fruit of any North American bird. Up to 84 percent of its diet are cedar, holly, and hawthorn berries and crabapple fruit. Also eats sap, flower petals, and insects. Moves long distances only when food sources run out. Gregarious in nature, waxwings band together for foraging and protection. Flocks containing several to a few hundred birds may feed side by side in winter, then rapidly disperse, startling potential predators. Call is a high-pitched, trilled *zeeeee*.

Habitat

Found in a variety of open habitats wherever fruit and berries are available.

Local Sites

Inhabiting cities, towns, parks, and gardens, Cedar Waxwings are present regionwide and year-round wherever food is abundant. Look for wandering groups in treetops during the fall, when flock sizes increase.

FIELD NOTES One of the more courteous diners in the bird world, Cedar Waxwings have been known to perch side by side and pass a piece of food down the row, one bird to the next, until one of them decides to eat it. If the bird at the end of the line receives the morsel and is disinclined as well, it is passed right back up the line.

Immature | "Myrtle"

YELLOW-RUMPED WARBLER

Dendroica coronata L 5.3" (13 cm)

FIELD MARKS
Bright yellow rump; yellow patch on sides of breast; pale eyebrow; white throat and sides of neck

Winter birds grayish brown above, white below with brown streaking

Breeding birds have yellow patch on crown, grayish blue upperparts

Behavior
The most abundant winter warbler in the Carolinas, it darts about branches from tree to tree or in bushes, foraging for myrtle berries and seeds. Often seen in winter in small foraging flocks. Will switch to primarily insect diet before spring migration. Songs of the eastern subspecies, the "Myrtle Warbler," include a slow warble and a musical trill. Call is a low, flat *check*.

Habitat
Common in fall and winter in brushy and wooded habitats, especially at field edges and on barrier islands. Seeks out areas rich in bayberry or juniper thickets.

Local Sites
Although migrant and wintering birds may be found regionwide, nowhere is it more common than in bayberry thickets of Assateague Island from October to March.

FIELD NOTES While these birds are preparing to leave for northerly breeding grounds around April, look for the male's bright breeding plumage (inset), characterized by a yellow crown patch and grayish blue upperparts. The female has a smaller crown patch and dusky brown upperparts.

Year-round | Adult male

AMERICAN REDSTART

Setophaga ruticilla L 5.3" (13 cm)

FIELD MARKS

Male is glossy black above and on hood; bright orange patches on sides, wings, and tail

Female gray-olive above; orange patches replaced with yellow

White belly and undertail coverts

Behavior

Often fans tail and spreads wings when perched. Darts suddenly to snare flying insects. Also takes insects, caterpillars, spiders, berries, fruit, and seeds from branches and foliage. Nests in forks of trees or bushes generally 10 to 20 feet from the ground. Song is a highly variable series of high, thin notes usually followed by a single, wheezy, downslurred note: *zee zee zee zee zweeah*. Calls include a thin, squeaky *chip* and a clear, penetrating *seep* in flight.

Habitat

Found in moist deciduous and mixed woodlands with thick undergrowth; also in wooded riparian zones and second-growth woodlands.

Local Sites

The Patuxent Research Refuge or New Germany State Park are likely locations in breeding season. Up to 100 a day may be seen in September at Assateague Island.

FIELD NOTES The Black-and-white Warbler, *Mniotilta varia* (inset: female), is identified by behavior as easily as by plumage. No other warbler has its nuthatch-like foraging style, creeping along branches and trunks. Breeds region-wide; especially common as a migrant, spring and fall.

Year-round | Adult male

PROTHONOTARY WARBLER

Protonotaria citrea L 5.5" (14 cm)

FIELD MARKS

Male's head and underparts
golden yellow; female duller

Blue-gray wings

Blue-gray tail has white patches;
white undertail coverts

Large dark eyes; long black bill

Behavior

Deliberate in plucking insects, larvae, spiders, and seeds
from crevices in ground, logs, and trees. Also picks
snails and crustaceans right out of water. After arriving
on breeding grounds and building several partial nests,
male sings incessantly until female arrives and chooses
a nest to complete. Song is a series of loud, ringing
zweet notes; call is a dry *chip*.

Habitat

Common in moist lowland forests, woodlands prone to
flooding, and stream banks, but wanders far during
migration. Unlike most warblers, nests in tree cavities,
nest boxes, or similar crannies, always near water.

Local Sites

Although Prothonotary is found along wooded rivers
in much of Maryland, the Pocomoke River hosts the
largest population by far. A May canoe trip can tally
over 100 birds in a morning!

FIELD NOTES The Yellow Warbler, *Dendroica petechia*
(inset), shares with the Prothonotary a prominent
dark eye, a bright yellow face, and a preference
for wet habitats, but not forests. The male Yellow
(inset, top), has red streaks on its breast.

Year-round | Adult male

COMMON YELLOWTHROAT

Geothlypis trichas L 5" (13 cm)

FIELD MARKS

Adult male shows broad, black mask bordered above by light gray

Female lacks black mask, has whitish patch around eyes

Grayish olive upperparts; bright yellow throat and breast; pale yellow undertail coverts

Behavior

Generally remains close to the ground, skulking and hiding in undergrowth. May also be seen climbing vertically on stems and singing from exposed perches. While foraging, cocks tail and hops on ground to glean insects, caterpillars, and spiders from foliage, twigs, and reeds. Nests atop piles of weeds and grass, or in small shrubs. One version of variable song is a loud, rolling *wichity wichity wichity wichity wich.* Calls include a husky *tshep,* a rapid chatter, and a buzzy *dzip* in flight.

Habitat

Stays low in marshes, shrubby fields, woodland edges, and thickets near water.

Local Sites

Abundant at virtually all lakes, ponds, and fields in the region, these warblers are easy to find at Blackwater National Wildlife Refuge and Hughes Hollow.

FIELD NOTES The largest North American warbler at 7.5", the Yellow-breasted Chat, *Icteria virens* (inset: male), is also an elusive skulker. Like the yellowthroat, it remains low to the ground, hidden in dense vegetation. Listen for its harsh, jumbled, unmusical song, given from a perch or in flight.

Year-round | Adult male

HOODED WARBLER

Wilsonia citrina L 5.3" (13 cm)

FIELD MARKS
Bright yellow face bordered by
black hood on male

Female shows variable amount of
black around yellow face

Olive-green above, yellow below
with white undertail

Behavior
Constantly opens and closes its tail feathers, revealing
white spots on the corners of its tail, as it forages low in
trees and shrubs or on the ground for insects, caterpillars, and spiders. Female builds nest of leaves, plant
material, spider silk, and fur; nest located low in shrubs
or small trees. Male sings persistently, but often from a
concealed perch, a clear, whistled *ta-wee ta-wee ta-wee
ta-wee tee-too,* with an emphatic ending. Call given by
both sexes is a loud *chink.*

Habitat
Tends to remain close to the ground, often hidden, in
thick understory of mature deciduous forests.

Local Sites
Mature forest understory of Patuxent River Park or
Green Ridge are areas with good numbers of Hooded
Warblers, though seeing them is always a challenge.

FIELD NOTES The Kentucky Warbler, *Oporornis
formosus* (inset: male), like the Hooded, has
bright yellow underparts and olive-green upperparts, but is distinguished by yellow spectacles sep-
arating the black on its crown from the black on its
face and neck. Both species largely remain hidden
in overgrowth, so listen for the Kentucky's low *chup*
call and for its song, a rolling, repeated *churree.*

Breeding | Adult male

SCARLET TANAGER

Piranga olivacea L 7" (18 cm)

FIELD MARKS

Breeding male has bright red
body and black wings and tail; 1st
spring male has browner wings

Female is olive above with darker
wings and tail, and yellow below

Fall adult male resembles female

Behavior

Forages for insects, berries, and fruit mostly high in the
tops of trees, but will also take food from the ground or
snag insects on the fly. Courtship display consists of
male perching below prospective mate and spreading
his wings to reveal his scarlet back. Male's song is
robinlike but raspier, given to defend territory and
attract a mate: *querit queer querry querit queer*. Female
sings a similar song, but softer and shorter. Call is a
hoarse *chip* or *chip-burr*.

Habitat

This resident of the forest interior is found in almost
any mature woodland that is not heavily fragmented.

Local Sites

Found in deciduous woodland regionwide. Particularly good areas are Patuxent Wildlife Research Refuge,
the C & O Canal Towpath, and Rocky Gap State Park.

FIELD NOTES Summer Tanagers, *Piranga rubra*
(inset: male), are often found in pine, also open
oak, forests of the Eastern Shore and southern
Maryland. Male Summers lack the Scarlet's
black wings; females have a more orange cast
and a larger bill than female Scarlets.

Year-round | Adult male

EASTERN TOWHEE

Pipilo erythrophthalmus L 7.5" (19 cm)

FIELD MARKS

Male has black hood, upperparts

Female similarly patterned, but black areas replaced by brown

Rufous sides; white underparts

White corners on long tail

Juvenile streaked light brown

Behavior

Stays low to the ground, scratching leaf litter frequently with feet together, head held low, and tail up, exposing prey such as seeds and insects. Also forages for grasshoppers, spiders, moths, and fruit. Male fans his wings and tail during courtship, displaying contrasting white patches on his primaries and tertials. Nests on the ground, near shrubs. Sings from an exposed perch a loud, ringing *drink your tea,* sometimes shortened to *drink tea.* Also calls in an emphatic, upslurred *chewink.*

Habitat

Prefers second-growth woodlands with dense shrubs, brushy thickets, and extensive leaf litter. Also found in brambly fields, suburban hedgerows, riparian areas, and forest clearings.

Local Sites

Common in virtually all forests and small woodlands, the towhee is especially easily seen at Assateague Island, where it scavenges campsites.

FIELD NOTES The juvenile Eastern Towhee has a brown cap, wings, and tail, and is heavily streaked with brown, which is especially distinct on its buff underparts. Look for one trailing its parents, only between May and August.

Breeding | Adult

CHIPPING SPARROW

Spizella passerina L 5.5" (14 cm)

FIELD MARKS
Breeding adult shows bright chestnut crown, white eyebrow, gray cheek and nape

Winter adult has streaked brown crown and a brown face

Streaked brown wings and back; unstreaked gray breast and belly

Behavior
Forages on the ground for insects, caterpillars, spiders, and seeds. May be found foraging in small family flocks in late summer. Known to employ the clever strategy of landing atop a reed so as to bend it by the force of its weight and more easily extract seeds from the reed tip. Nests close to the ground in branches or vine tangles. Sings from a high perch a one-pitched, rapid-fire trill of dry *chip* notes. Call in flight is a sharp *tseet*, otherwise a high *tsip*.

Habitat
Found in suburban parks and gardens, woodland edges and clearings; prefers conifers when breeding.

Local Sites
Abundant in cities, towns, and woodlands, Chipping Sparrows can be seen in spring and summer at New Germany and Susquehanna State Parks, as well as in many backyards.

FIELD NOTES Populating many of the same open woodlands and fields as the Chipping Sparrow, the Field Sparrow, *Spizella pusilla* (inset), is widespread in the region year-round. Its gray face, light brown crown, and buffy breast and flanks distinguish it from the Chipping, as well as its pink bill and distinct white eye ring.

Year-round | Adult

SAVANNAH SPARROW

Passerculus sandwichensis L 5.5" (14 cm)

FIELD MARKS

Yellow or whitish eyebrow

Pale median crown stripe on streaked crown

Dark brown streaked upperparts

White below with brown streaking on chin, breast, and flanks

Behavior

Forages on the ground singly or in a pair for insects, spiders, and seeds in spring and summer. Forms loose flocks in migration and winter that feed primarily on seeds and berries. Sometimes scratches in dirt like a towhee. Nests on the ground in small depression concealed by grasses. Song begins with two or three *chip* notes, followed by long buzzy trill and a final *tip* note. Common call is a high *tip*. Flight call is a thin, descending *tseew*.

Habitat

Found in a variety of open habitats, such as grasslands, farm fields, and pastures.

Local Sites

Migrates regionwide. Winters in Worcester County, other Eastern Shore locales. In breeding season, try Garrett County south of Oakland.

FIELD NOTES Savannah Sparrow has a number of subspecies across its wide range. One of the most distinctive is the large, very pale "Ipswich Sparrow," *Passerculus sandwichensis princeps*. Its small population breeds only on Cape Sable Island, Nova Scotia, and winters only on Atlantic beaches. Assateague Island lies at the center of its winter range and has produced record-high tallies for the annual Christmas Bird Count.

Year-round | Adult

SONG SPARROW

Melospiza melodia L 6.3" (16 cm)

FIELD MARKS

Underparts whitish, with streaks
on sides and breast that converge
into a dark breast spot

Streaked brown and gray above;
broad, grayish eyebrow; broad,
dark malar stripe

Long, rounded tail

Behavior

Forages in trees and bushes and on ground for insects,
larvae, seeds, and berries, sometimes scratching ground
to unearth food. Nests on the ground or near it in trees
and bushes. Female broods young while male defends
territory intently, singing from exposed perch and bat-
tling competitors. Belts out a melodious song, three
to four short, clear notes followed by a buzzy *tow-wee*,
then a trill. Common call is a nasal, hollow *chimp*.
Flight call is a clear, rising *seeet*.

Habitat

Common in suburban and rural gardens, weedy fields,
dense streamside thickets, and forest edges.

Local Sites

Find the Song Sparrow in suburban backyards or local
parks year-round anywhere in the region.

FIELD NOTES The larger Fox Sparrow,
Passerella iliaca (inset), appears throughout
the region in migration and in the eastern half
in winter. It remains close to the ground, sometimes foraging like a towhee, but it prefers more
densely wooded areas. Compared to Song, it is larger, has
a yellow bill base, is much more rufous overall, and its breast
streaking converges into a large central splotch.

Year-round | Adult

WHITE-THROATED SPARROW

Zonotrichia albicollis L 6.8" (17 cm)

FIELD MARKS

Broad eyebrow is yellow in front of eye, white or tan behind

Black lateral crown stripes and eye lines; white throat bordered by gray

Streaked rusty brown above, grayish below

Behavior

Employs double-scratch foraging method, raking leaf litter with backward kick of both feet, keeping head held low and tail pointed up. Also forages in bushes and trees for seeds, tree buds, and insects. Nests close to or on ground, often at forest edges near water. Calls include a sharp *pink* and a drawn out, lisping *tseep,* given in flight. Its song, given year-round, is a thin whistle of one or two single notes then three or four longer notes: *pure sweet Canada Canada Canada.*

Habitat

Winters in woodland undergrowth, brush, and gardens. Breeds primarily in shrubby wetlands.

Local Sites

Although gone from the region in summer, the White-throated Sparrow is among the most common winter residents in brushy forest undergrowth. Commonly seen at backyard feeders.

FIELD NOTES Another migrant and winter visitor to the region is the White-crowned Sparrow, *Zonotrichia leucophrys* (inset). The White-crowned is distinguished by its lack of yellow in front of the eye and its grayish throat, not as clearly marked off from its breast. It prefers hedgerows and weedy fields over forests and brush.

Year-round | Adult male "Slate-colored"

DARK-EYED JUNCO

Junco hyemalis L 6.3" (16 cm)

FIELD MARKS

Dark gray hood and upperparts
on male, brownish on female

White outer tail feathers in flight

White belly and undertail coverts

Pale pinkish bill

Juvenile streaked brown overall

Behavior
Forages by scratching on ground to expose food and by gleaning seeds, grain, berries, insects, caterpillars, and fruit from vegetation. Occasionally gives chase to a flying insect. Forms flocks in winter, when males may stay farther north or at greater elevations than immatures and females. Nests on or close to ground, sheltered by a bush or in a cavity such as a tree root. Song, given year-round, is a short, musical trill on one pitch. Calls include a sharp *dit,* and a rapid twittering in flight.

Habitat
Winters in a wide variety of habitats, especially patchy wooded areas and including backyard feeding stations. Breeds in high-elevation mixed woodlands.

Local Sites
Nesting birds can be found on Garrett County ridges. Wintering birds are common at feeders and wood edges regionwide

---

FIELD NOTES Though widely scattered geographically and fairly different in their field marks, 12 subspecies of Dark-eyed Junco are recognized by the American Ornithologists' Union. A western form, the "Oregon" Junco, is an accidental vagrant rarely seen at feeding stations in the region in winter. It shows a black or dark hood, a reddish brown back, a gray rump, and a white belly.

Year-round | Adult male

NORTHERN CARDINAL

Cardinalis cardinalis L 8.8" (22 cm)

FIELD MARKS

Male is red overall; black on face

Female is buffy brown tinged with red on wings, crest, and tail

Large, conspicuous crest

Cone-shaped, reddish bill; blackish on juvenile

Behavior

Generally seen alone or in a pair in summer; in small groups in winter. Forages on the ground or low in shrubs for insects, seeds, leaf buds, berries, and fruit. Territorially aggressive, attacks not only other birds, but also itself, reflected in windows, rear-view mirrors, and chrome surfaces. Nests in forks of trees and bushes, or in tangles of twigs and vines. Call is a sharp, somewhat metallic *chip*. Sings a variety of melodious songs year-round, including a *cue cue cue,* a *cheer cheer cheer,* and a *purty purty purty.* Listen for courtship duets in spring.

Habitat

Found in gardens and parks, woodland edges, stream-side thickets, and practically any environment that provides thick, brushy cover. The cardinal has adapted so well to landscaped yards and backyard feeders that it continues to expand its range northward into Canada.

Local Sites

Cardinals are a year-round delight in backyards, parks, and every other habitat throughout the region.

FIELD NOTES Cardinals may appear sleek and streamlined in summer and plumper in winter. This is because, as with many birds, they fluff out their body feathers in colder months in order to create pockets of air that conserve body heat.

CARDINALS, GROSBEAKS, BUNTINGS

Year-round | Adult male

Passerina caerulea L 6.8" (17 cm)

FIELD MARKS

Adult male deep blue overall with black face and wide chestnut wing bars

Female dull brownish overall

Large, heavy bill; upper mandible darker than lower

Behavior

Groups of birds arrive in spring, but soon after disperse into pairs. Forages by hopping around on the ground for insects, snails, fruit, grain, and seeds. Will fly from perch to hawk insects in mid-air, and occasionally hovers to glean insects from leaves and twigs. Has a habit of twitching and spreading its tail. Distinctive call is a loud *chink*. Song is a full-bodied series of rising and falling warbles.

Habitat

Any low, brushy habitat along a stream, golf course, marsh, roadway, or woodland edge, especially one near water. Nests low in trees, bushes, or clumps of weeds.

Local Sites

Blue Grosbeaks breed in old fields and orchards region-wide, though they are rare in the far west. Blackwater National Wildlife Refuge and E. A. Vaughn Wildlife Management Area have high concentrations.

FIELD NOTES The Blue Grosbeak's cousin, the Rose-breasted Grosbeak, *Pheucticus ludovicianus* (inset: male), can be found in summer breeding in the Appalachians, or in spring or fall migrating throughout the region. Look for the male's rose-red breast on otherwise black-and-white plumage.

Breeding | Adult male

INDIGO BUNTING

Passerina cyanea L 5.5" (14 cm)

FIELD MARKS
Breeding male deep blue overall, darker on head; blackish wings

Female is brownish, with diffuse streaking on breast and flanks and a bluish tail

Fall male has varied amount of brown on back, breast, and lores

Behavior
Forages for insects and larvae from ground level to canopy in spring and summer, switching to a seed and berry diet in the fall. Uses heavy conical bill to crack or hull seeds. Forms mixed-species flocks in migration and winter. Nests in shrubs or low in trees, using weeds, bark, grass, and leaves. Territorially aggressive males will often chase away other males. Call is a dry, metallic *pik*. Sings from high perch a series of varied phrases, usually doubled. Second-year males appear to learn songs from competing males, not from parents.

Habitat
Prefers forest edges and bushy transition zones between fields or clearcuts and second-growth woodlands.

Local Sites
Found commonly regionwide in spring and summer, male Indigos sing from elevated perches at Blackwater National Wildlife Refuge, Rocky Gap State Park, and Hughes Hollow.

FIELD NOTES The female Indigo Bunting (inset), with her brown back, buffy wing bars, and slightly streaked undersides, resembles a sparrow if seen alone. Look for her bluish tail, bicolored bill, and unstreaked head and back to tell her apart.

Year-round | Adult male

RED-WINGED BLACKBIRD

Agelaius phoeniceus L 8.8" (22 cm)

FIELD MARKS

Male is glossy black with bright red shoulder patches broadly edged in buffy yellow

Females densely streaked overall

Pointed black bill

Wings slightly rounded at tips

Behavior
Runs and hops while foraging for insects, seeds, and grains in pastures and open fields. Male reveals red shoulder patches when he sings from a perch, often atop a cattail or tall weed stalk. Territorially aggressive, a male's social status is dependent on the amount of red he displays. Nests colonially in cattails, bushes, or dense grass near water. Song is a hoarse, gurgling *konk-la-reee,* ending in a trill. Call is a low *chuk* note.

Habitat
Breeds mainly in freshwater marshes and wet fields with thick vegetation. During winter, flocks forage in wooded swamps and farm fields.

Local Sites
Any river or pond with a marshy edge is likely to host breeding Red-winged Blackbirds. Large marsh areas such as Elliott Island host them in abundance. Fall flocks of thousands gather at Jug Bay Wetlands Sanctuary, and wintering hordes frequent Eastern Shore farm fields.

FIELD NOTES Usually less visible within large flocks of singing males, the female Red-winged (inset) is streaked dark brown above and has dusky white underparts heavily streaked with dark brown. In winter you may find a whole flock of just females.

Year-round | Adult

EASTERN MEADOWLARK

Sturnella magna L 9.5" (24 cm)

FIELD MARKS

Yellow below, with black V-shaped breast band, obscured in winter

Black-and-whitish striped crown with yellow supraloral area

Brown above, streaked with black

White outer tail feathers

Behavior

Flicks tail open and shut while foraging on the ground. Feeds mainly on insects during spring and summer, seeds and grain in fall and winter. Forms small flocks in fall and winter. Female constructs a domed nest on the ground, often woven into the surrounding live grasses. Male known to brood while female starts second nest. Often perches on fence posts or telephone poles to sing three to five (and sometimes more) loud, descending whistles: *tsweee-tsweee-TSWEEEOOO.* Calls include a buzzy *dzert*, a high-pitched chatter, and a whistled *weeet* in flight.

Habitat

Prefers the open space offered by grasslands, pastures, meadows, farm fields, and large lawns.

Local Sites

Any sizeable grassy fields, such as those at Blackwater National Wildlife Refuge, will have meadowlarks. Meadowlarks also occur in upper edges of salt marshes at Elliott Island and elsewhere.

FIELD NOTES Hayfields of north central and western Maryland host the breeding Bobolink, *Dolichonyx oryzivorous* (inset: male). Females and winter males look like large, yellowish sparrows with bold black head stripes. In fall, flocks of hundreds gather to feed on wild rice in the region's marshes.

Year-round | Adult male

COMMON GRACKLE

Quiscalus quiscula L 12.6" (32 cm)

FIELD MARKS

Plumage appears all black; in good light, male shows glossy purplish hood, green back

Long, wedge-shaped tail

Pale yellow eyes

Narrow, pointed beak

Behavior

Usually seen in a flock, this grackle moves to large, noisy, communal roosts in the evening. During the day, mainly seen on the ground in a group, feeding on insects, spiders, grubs, and earthworms. Also wades into shallow water to forage for minnows and crayfish. Known to feast on eggs and baby birds. Courtship display consists of male puffing out shoulder feathers to make a collar, drooping his wings, and singing. These birds produce sounds like ripping cloth or cracking twigs. Call note is a loud *chuck*.

Habitat

Prefers open spaces provided by farm fields, pastures, marshes, and suburban yards. Requires wooded areas, especially conifers, for nesting and roosting.

Local Sites

Common Grackles are abundant and gregarious year-round throughout the region.

FIELD NOTES The closely related Boat-tailed Grackle, *Quiscalus major* (inset: male), is larger than the Common Grackle and has different calls. Look for its long, keel-shaped tail along the coast and in lower Chesapeake Bay salt marshes.

Year-round | Adult male

BROWN-HEADED COWBIRD

Molothrus ater L 7.5" (19 cm)

FIELD MARKS

Male's brown head contrasts with metallic black body

Female gray-brown above, paler below with a whitish throat

Short, dark, pointed bill

Juvenile streaked below

Behavior

Often forages on the ground among herds of cattle, feeding on insects flushed by the grazing animals. Also feeds heavily on seeds and grain. Generally cocks its tail up while feeding. A nest parasite, it will wander for many miles to lay its eggs in the nests of other species, leaving the responsibilities of feeding and fledging of young to the host birds. Primary song is a series of liquid, purring gurgles followed by a high whistle: *bub ko lum tseeee.* Call is a soft *kek.* Females also give a dry chatter, while males emit a modulated whistle in flight.

Habitat

Found in open areas such as farmlands, pastures, forest edges, and lawns. Also seen around human habitation.

Local Sites

These birds breed throughout the region in virtually every city, town, field, and farm. Large flocks spend the winter with blackbirds and grackles at farmlands of the Eastern Shore.

FIELD NOTES The Brown-headed Cowbird flourishes in most of North America, adapting to newly cleared lands and exposing new songbirds—now more than 200 species—to its parasitic brooding habit. The female Brown-headed Cowbird lays up to 40 eggs a season in the nests of host birds, leaving the task of raising her young to the host species.

Year-round | Adult male

BALTIMORE ORIOLE

Icterus galbula L 8.3" (21 cm)

FIELD MARKS

Male has black hood and back; bright orange rump and under-parts; large orange patches on tail

Female is olive-brown above, orange below, with some black on head and throat

Black wings with white edging

Behavior

Mainly eats caterpillars, but will feed as well on other insects, berries, fruit, even flower nectar. Forages high in bushes and trees. Male bows to female, with wings and tail spread, during courtship. Suspends its bag-shaped nest near the tip of a tree branch about 30 feet up, an adaptation designed to deter egg-eating snakes and mammals. Calls include a whistled *hew-li* and a dry chatter. Song is a variable series of sweet, musical whistles.

Habitat

Breeds in deciduous woodlands and wooded suburbs. In migration, found wherever there are tall trees.

Local Sites

Maryland's state bird, Baltimore Orioles breed region-wide but are most prevalent in the western half. The C & O Canal Towpath, Lilypons Water Gardens, or Rocky Gap State Park are all good locations.

FIELD NOTES Sharing much of the same breeding grounds as the Baltimore Oriole, the Orchard Oriole, *Icterus spurius,* spends most of its time in open woodlands, farmlands, and orchards. The male (inset, bottom) has a black hood and chestnut underparts. The female (inset, top) is olive above and yellow below with dusky wings.

Year-round | Adult male

HOUSE FINCH

Carpodacus mexicanus L 6" (15 cm)

FIELD MARKS

Male's forehead, bib, and rump are typically red, but can be orange or, occasionally, yellow

Brown streaked back, pale belly, streaked flanks

Female streaked dusky brown on entire body

Behavior

Forages on the ground in fields and suburban yards primarily for seeds, sometimes for insects or fruit. Often visits backyard feeders. Seen in large mixed-species flocks during winter. Flies in undulating pattern, during which squared-off tail is evident. Builds cup-like nest on buildings, in shrubs or trees, or on the ground. Male sings a lively, high-pitched song consisting of varied three-note phrases, usually ending in a nasal *wheeer*. Most common call is a whistled *wheat*.

Habitat

Adaptable to varied habitats, these birds are found abundantly in shrubby areas near human habitation, including urban and suburban parks.

Local Sites

A western species, House Finches first reached Maryland in 1958. They are now ubiquitous breeders in every habitat, including urban areas.

FIELD NOTES The Purple Finch, *Carpodacus purpureus,* is not purple but rose-red on the body of the adult male (inset, bottom). The female (inset, top) is gray-brown above and heavily streaked below, with a bolder face pattern and a more deeply notched tail than the House Finch. Purple Finch is much less common, but may be seen with House Finches at winter feeders.

Breeding | Adult male

AMERICAN GOLDFINCH

Carduelis tristis L 5" (13 cm)

FIELD MARKS

Breeding male is bright yellow with black cap; female and winter male duller overall, lacking cap

Black wings with white bars

Black and white tail; white undertail coverts

Behavior

Gregarious and active. Large winter flocks may include several other species. Typical goldfinch diet, mostly seeds, is the most vegetarian of any North American bird, though the goldfinch does sometimes eat insects as well. During courtship, male performs exaggerated, undulating aerial maneuvers, and often feeds the incubating female. Nests at forest edges or in old fields, often late in summer after thistles have bloomed so they can be used as nest lining and seeds as food for young. Song is a lively series of trills, twitters, and *swee* notes. Calls include a distinctive *per-chik-o-ree,* and a descending *ti-di-di-di,* given mainly in flight.

Habitat

Found in weedy fields, open woodlands, and anywhere rich in thistles and sunflowers.

Local Sites

These birds are common year-round in city parks, suburbs, and farm fields with scattered trees, everywhere in the region except the thickest forests.

FIELD NOTES The nonbreeding male goldfinch (inset) loses his black cap except for a spot just above the bill and molts into much drabber yellowish brown plumage. The nonbreeding female is similar, but an even drabber grayish overall.

Breeding | Adult male

HOUSE SPARROW

Passer domesticus L 6.3" (16 cm)

FIELD MARKS

Breeding male has black bill, bib, and lores; chestnut eye stripes, nape, back, and shoulders

Winter male less patterned

Female has brown back, streaked with black; buffy eyestripe; and unstreaked grayish breast

Behavior

Abundant and gregarious. Hops around, feeding on grain, seeds, and shoots, or seeks out bird feeders for sunflower seeds and millet. In urban areas, begs for food from humans and will clean up any crumbs left behind. In spring and summer, multiple suitors will chase a possible mate in high-speed aerial pursuit. Females choose mate mostly according to song display. Nests in any sheltered cavity; often usurping it, then vigorously defending it, from other species. Singing males give persistent *chirp* notes. Calls are variable.

Habitat

Found in close proximity to humans. Can be seen in urban and suburban areas and in rural landscapes inhabited by humans and livestock.

Local Sites

From big-city streets to isolated farms, these abundant breeders are found anywhere that people live.

FIELD NOTES Also known as the English Sparrow, the House Sparrow was first introduced into New York City in 1851 in an effort to control insect pests. It has since spread across the continent to become one of the most successful bird species in North America, to the detriment of many native species. Ironically, its numbers are declining precipitously in its native England.

Color categories reflect the overall colors of a species, not just the head color. Where sexes or ages differ, we typically show the most colorful plumage.

Mostly Blue

Mostly Brown

Mostly Brown and White

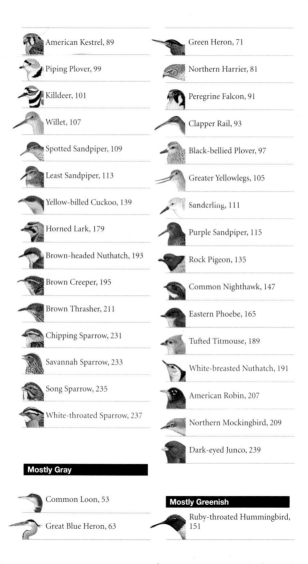

Mostly Gray

Mostly Greenish

The first entry page number for each species is listed in **boldface** type and refers to the text page opposite the illustration. A check-off box is provided next to each common-name entry so that you can use this index as a checklist of the species you have identified.

ACKNOWLEDGMENTS

The Book Division would like to thank the following people for their guidance and contribution in creating the *National Geographic Field Guide to Birds: Maryland and Washington, D.C.*

Cortez C. Austin, Jr.:
Cortez Austin is a wildlife photographer specializing in North American and tropical birds. An ardent conservationist, he has donated images, given lectures, and written book reviews for a wide variety of conservation organizations. In addition, he has published numerous articles and photographs in birding magazines, field guides, and wildlife books.

Richard Crossley:
Richard Crossley is an Englishman obsessed by birding since age 10. He traveled the world studying birds but fell in love with Cape May while pioneering the identification of overhead warbler migration in 1985. He is co-author of *The Shorebird Guide*, due in Spring 2006.

Bates Littlehales:
A National Geographic photographer for more than 30 years covering myriad subjects around the globe, Bates Littlehales continues to specialize in photographing birds and is an expert in capturing their beauty and ephemeral nature. Bates is co-author of the *National Geographic Photographic Field Guide: Birds*, and a contributor to the *National Geographic Reference Atlas to the Birds of North America*.

Brian E. Small:
Brian E. Small is a full-time professional wildlife photographer specializing in birds, as well as a regular columnist and Advisory Board member for *WildBird* magazine. Brian is currently Photo Editor for the American Birding Association's *Birding* magazine. You can find more of his images at www.briansmallphoto.com.

Tom Vezo:
Tom Vezo is an award-winning wildlife photographer who is widely published throughout the U.S. and Europe. He specializes in bird photography but photographs other wildlife and nature subjects as well. He is a contributor to the *National Geographic Reference Atlas to the Birds of North America*. Please visit Tom at www.tomvezo.com.

Photography

Cortez C. Austin, Jr.: pp. 16, 20, 36, 42, 54, 56, 84, 158, 192, 250. **Tom Brakefield/CORBIS:** p. 46. **Richard Crossley:** pp. 92, 182. **Mike Danzenbaker:** p. 116. **Marshall J. Iliff:** p. 84. **Bates Littlehales:** pp. 112, 208, 212, 218, 224. **Larry Sansone:** p. 148. **Rulon E. Simmons:** p. 64. **Brian E. Small:** pp. Cover, 30, 32, 34, 38, 40, 58, 62, 66, 72, 88, 90, 102, 104, 106, 114, 120, 138, 140, 142, 150, 156, 166, 168, 176, 178, 180, 186, 188, 190, 194, 202, 204, 206, 210, 216, 226, 230, 232, 234, 238, 260. **Bob Steele:** pp. 2, 68. **TomVezo.com:** pp. 14, 18, 22, 24, 26, 28, 44, 48, 50, 52, 60, 70, 74, 76, 78, 80, 82, 86, 94, 96, 98, 100, 108, 110, 122, 124, 126, 128, 130, 132, 134, 136, 144, 146, 152, 154, 160, 162, 164, 170, 172, 174, 184, 196, 200, 214, 220, 228, 236, 240, 242, 246, 248, 252, 254, 256, 258, 262. **Garth McElroy/VIREO:** p. 198. **Rob & Ann Simpson/VIREO:** p. 222. **T.J. Ulrich/VIREO:** p. 118.

Artwork

Jonathan Alderfer: 10 (bottom), 97, 117. **David Beadle:** 9. **Peter Burke:** 73, 223, 227, 229, 255. **Marc R. Hanson:** 93, 95. **Cynthia J. House:** 15, 19, 25, 27, 29, 31, 33, 35, 37, 43, 45, 47. **H. Jon Janosik:** 55, 59, 61. **Donald L. Malick:** 75, 79, 83, 91, 141, 145, 155, 159. **John P. O'Neill:** 187. **Kent Pendleton:** 49. **Diane Pierce:** 10 (top), 67, 69, 231, 235, 237, 243, 245, 257, 259. **John C. Pitcher:** 99, 109, 115. **H. Douglas Pratt:** 135, 139, 151, 165, 171, 185, 191, 199, 201, 209, 217, 219, 225, 247, 251. **David Quinn:** 53. **Chuck Ripper:** 147. **N. John Schmitt:** 85. **Thomas R. Schultz:** 10 (middle), 111, 119, 121, 125, 127, 129, 205, 221, 249.

NATIONAL GEOGRAPHIC
FIELD GUIDE TO BIRDS:
MARYLAND & WASHINGTON, D.C.

Edited by Jonathan Alderfer

**Published by
the National Geographic Society**

John M. Fahey, Jr.,
President and Chief Executive Officer

Gilbert M. Grosvenor,
Chairman of the Board

Nina D. Hoffman,
*Executive Vice President;
President, Books & School Publishing*

Prepared by the Book Division

Kevin Mulroy,
Senior Vice President and Publisher

Kristin Hanneman, *Illustrations Director*

Marianne R. Koszorus, *Design Director*

Carl Mehler, *Director of Maps*

Barbara Brownell Grogan,
Executive Editor

Staff for this Book

Barbara Levitt, *Editor*

Kate Griffin, *Illustrations Editor*

Alexandra Littlehales, *Designer*

Carol Norton, *Series Art Director*

Suzanne Poole, *Text Editor*

Teresa Tate, *Illustrations Specialist*

Abby Leopold, *Illustrations Coordinator*

Marshall Iliff, *Map Research*

Matt Chwastyk, Sven M. Dolling,
Map Production

Michael Greninger, *Editorial Assistant*

Rick Wain, *Production Project Manager*

Manufacturing and Quality Control

Christopher A. Liedel,
Chief Financial Officer

Phillip L. Schlosser, *Managing Director*

John T. Dunn, *Technical Director*

One of the world's largest nonprofit scientific and educational organizations, the National Geographic Society was founded in 1888 "for the increase and diffusion of geographic knowledge." Fulfilling this mission, the Society educates and inspires millions every day through its magazines, books, television programs, videos, maps and atlases, research grants, the National Geographic Bee, teacher workshops, and innovative classroom materials. The Society is supported through membership dues, charitable gifts, and income from the sale of its educational products. This support is vital to National Geographic's mission to increase global understanding and promote conservation of our planet through exploration, research, and education.

For more information, please call 1-800-NGS LINE (647-5463) or write to the following address:

National Geographic Society
1145 17th Street N.W.
Washington, D.C. 20036-4688 U.S.A.

Log on to nationalgeographic.com;
AOL Keyword: NatGeo

For information about special discounts for bulk purchases, please contact National Geographic Books Special Sales.
ngspecsales@ngs.org

**Library of Congress
Cataloging-in-Publication Data**

Available upon request.

ISBN-10: 1-4262-0007-2

ISBN-13: 978-1-4262-0007-6